Christmas 2003

May the rich joys of Jesus
fill your heart and home
during this holiday season,
and throughout the coming
year!

Blessings,
Steve & Becky Witmer

Love
Found
a Way

Love Found a Way

Ron Mehl

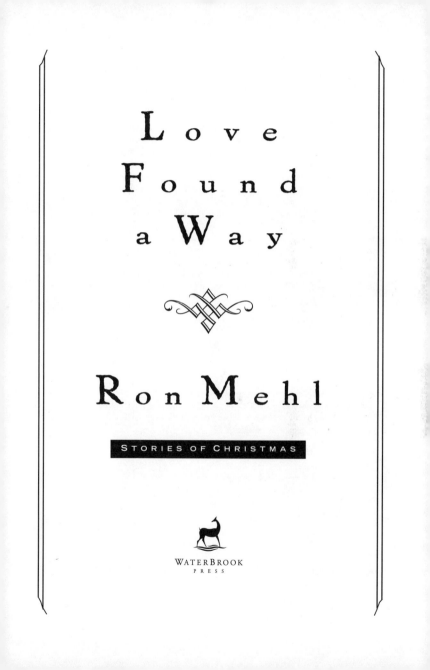

STORIES OF CHRISTMAS

WATERBROOK
PRESS

LOVE FOUND A WAY
PUBLISHED BY WATERBROOK PRESS
5446 North Academy Boulevard, Suite 200
Colorado Springs, Colorado 80918
A division of Random House, Inc.

ISBN 1-57856-276-7

Library of Congress Cataloging-in-Publication Data
Mehl, Ron.
     Love found a way : stories of Christmas / Ron Mehl.—1st ed.
         p.   cm.
     ISBN 1-57856-276-7
     1. Christmas Meditations.   I. Title.
BV45.M44   1999
242'.335—dc21   99-33692
                                                       CIP

Printed in the United States of America
1999—First Edition

10 9 8 7 6 5 4 3 2 1

To
JOYCE, RON JR., ELIZABETH,
MARK, STEPHANIE, AND LIESL...

*who have found so many ways to show
the gift of love to me and others*

Contents

Acknowledgments

Many things that we do require a great deal of work. A lot of the projects we have seem difficult, if not impossible. The point is we all need help. My mom always used to say, "Don't worry; we'll find a way."

First, I find myself greatly indebted to Jesus, who, because of His love, found a way to save us.

I'm also very thankful for the people who were touched enough by the subject of "Love found a way" that they encouraged me to do this.

To Dan Rich and the WaterBrook family, I am extremely thankful. Bless you for the confidence you've shown in me.

I want to say a large thank-you to two pastor friends: Joe Wittwer, from Spokane, Washington, who gave me some very helpful and moving insights; and to Amos Dodge, from Washington, D.C., who is a reservoir of godly wisdom and love. To both of them, I say thanks.

I'd like to express heartfelt thanks to Peggie Bates, Gayle Potter, Betty Martin, and Debbie Matheny, for their work in typing and reading (and typing and reading), and for keeping my life in order.

I am indebted to the editing team of Larry Libby and

Steve Halliday, for their commitment to *Love Found a Way*. Larry is one of the most influential people in my life. The addition of Steve Halliday makes me wonder why God blesses me so much. Larry and Steve are both highly regarded editors and writers. I feel humbled they would work with me.

Finally (and most of all), I would like to express gratitude to my wife, Joyce, who has shown me that love is more than words; it's action. Love always finds a way.

WINTER
BY
ROBIN MOLINE

A Personal Note

Some people think I get a little carried away with Christmas. No, they don't actually *say* anything (who wants to offend the pastor?). But I can tell. I've caught them rolling their eyes or changing the subject. I know what they're thinking. They think I'm too sentimental and nostalgic. All right, I confess. I *do* love the trees, decorations, carols, gifts, lights, candy— and all the rest of it. And if I'm "carried away," at least it's to somewhere I want to go!

But that's not the reason for my enthusiasm and joy.

This time of year never fails to excite me because God, the real gift-giver, found a way to love, bless, and care for people like me. While the world has made Christmas a brazenly commercial, nonsacred event, I refuse to become cynical or to allow what others do to strip My Favorite Day of its true meaning.

For me, the bells I hear at Christmas announce the glorious truth that God so loved the world that He gave His only begotten Son. They say Christmas is for children, and from my earliest memories Mom taught me that Christmas was about a person…a baby born in a manger who grew up to love, heal, and ultimately give His life to save the lost. This Christmas, He lives to rule and reign on our behalf.

When you stop to think about it, that first Christmas took a bit of doing. The organization, forethought, and planning that had to take place makes my head spin. But love found a way, didn't it?

I can remember one Christmas when I was trying to put together a bookshelf/entertainment center all-in-one kind of deal out in the garage. My wife, Joyce, had said, "Can you put this thing together?"

"Of course I can," I answered. (What else could I say and maintain my masculine dignity?) After about four and a half hours, however, I can assure you I was not humming "O Holy Night." In fact, I was fit to be tied. In spite of my best efforts, I had evidently messed everything up to a shocking degree. Nothing would work. The screws were the wrong size. The holes were too small. The corners didn't fit. Finally, in frustration, I called Joyce for help.

She began by asking if I'd looked at the directions. What a question! Everyone knows that directions are only the last resort of dexterity-challenged individuals. But because I'd asked her to help me, we looked. As it turned out, the instructions were pretty simple. "Start with A, then go to B, C," and so on. It took us a while to get to Z, but we got there.

When it came to that first Christmas, God said, "I'll put everything together. It will take some work, but I'll do it." In Isaiah, the prophet writes: "For a child is born to us, a son is given to us. And the government will rest on his shoulders. These will be his royal titles: Wonderful Counselor, Mighty God, Everlasting Father, Prince of Peace. His ever expanding peaceful government will never end. He will rule forever with fairness and justice from the throne of his ancestor David. *The passionate commitment of the LORD Almighty will guarantee this!*" (Isaiah 9:6-7, NLT, emphasis mine).

Israel was in the midst of distress and great affliction, and her people needed hope and a deliverer. They couldn't put everything together either. They needed help. God said, "A child will be born, and He will be My gift of life to you." And God added, "I'm committed to making this happen. I won't let anything get in the way of My Christmas plans."

And nothing did. It all happened right on schedule. God made sure everything was ready when it had to be ready. The Bible calls it, "the fullness of time." From Mary and Joseph arriving in Bethlehem to the shepherds in the fields, the angels in the heavens, and a bright star in the sky, God's love found a way to package it all in just the right way at just the right moment. "The passionate commitment of the LORD Almighty will guarantee this."

Realizing that God held back nothing, pulled out all the stops, and used the mighty resources of heaven to give the greatest gift of all ought to give us fresh reason to celebrate

His birth—no matter how the world tries to twist or gloss over the truth. When we make the Lord Jesus the focus, our holidays really do become "holy days." Sure, some will try to make it into a pagan ritual. Maybe they just don't know the score. Maybe you and I could help them discover the true and eternal purpose and meaning of Christmas.

Love will find a way.

CHAPTER ONE

Love Found a Way

*For God so loved the world that he gave
his one and only Son.*

JOHN 3:16

For the words "Love Found a Way" to mean anything, we have to first reckon with the fact that there was no way.

No way for a glorious, holy God to relate to fallen men and women.

No way to enjoy God's companionship and wisdom.

No way to tap into His grace and power.

No way for sins to be forgiven.

No way to escape judgment.

No way to achieve heaven.

Christmas reminds us in its own quiet and surprising way that God has little use for the phrase, "No way!" When there appears to be no way out of trouble and no way into blessing; when we can see no way to win and no way to avoid losing; when circumstances beat down our hopes and drown out our cries with their loud, mocking shouts of "No way!"—just then God steps into the picture, and at the foot of the manger says softly but irresistibly,

> With man this is impossible, but with God all
> things are possible. (Matthew 19:26)

Amid all the glittery, tinselly, flashy things that so often capture our attention at Christmastime, perhaps we could pause and take some time to recall that the Baby of Bethlehem came to be with us for a reason. He came to die so that we could live our lives with hope.

As Ephesians tells us, you and I were "separate from Christ, excluded from citizenship in Israel and foreigners to the covenants of the promise, without hope and without God in the world. But now in Christ Jesus [we] who once were far away have been brought near through the blood of Christ" (Ephesians 2:12-13).

Brought near.

Love found a way to do the undoable and to reach the unreachable. Love found a way when there was no way.

Isn't that what Christmas is all about? When we contemplate what His love did for us, we find our hearts exploding and our spirits soaring at the dizzying thought of the new, dazzling future that lies open before us—a future full of possibility and joy and hope and delight and great surprise. No wonder that those who find creative ways to remember the way-making God always seem to be the happiest, dearest people we meet!

Mama Clark's Christmas Tree

Mama Clark, a saintly woman of eighty, beamed with satisfaction as I loaded my plate from the heaping platters. After letting me eat a few bites, she turned to me with a distinct twinkle in her eyes.

"Pastor Ron," she said, "I just finished my Christmas tree. I really like it. I think this may be the best yet."

"Really?" I replied around a mouthful of baked ham. "Do you have special decorations?"

Did she ever.

I had been invited to speak in Amish country, outside of Dover, Ohio. Our little group sat down to a Christmas banquet at a huge Amish restaurant, packed with what seemed to be hundreds of people. Mama Clark had asked if I would sit by her, and of course I told her I would be honored.

What a feast! My new friends and I sat at a long table draped with a snow-white tablecloth. Once the food started coming, I thought it would never stop. Waitresses hurried in with heaping dishes of mashed potatoes dappled with pools of yellow butter. These were followed in succession by steaming platters of fried chicken and ham, huge bowls of corn and peas, and plates of hot biscuits, all served family style. When one bowl got low, it was immediately replaced with another. I don't think I've ever seen so much food on one table—and I'm quite sure my cholesterol count has never been the same since that day.

Mama Clark was absently nudging a pile of peas with her fork. She had other things on her mind besides food. "Oh, Pastor Ron," she said, "I just wish you could see my tree. I decorated it with a *wedding* theme."

"Really?"

I didn't know how to reply. *A wedding theme?* On a Christmas tree? Perhaps this dear elderly lady was beginning to lose her grip. "Tell me about it," I said.

While I applied strawberry preserves to a hot biscuit, Mama Clark explained that her tree this year featured wedding invitations, bride and groom pictures, tiny bags of rice, rings, personalized napkins, a miniature guest book, dainty white-wrapped presents, and little wedding cakes. It was all to illustrate, she told me, Jesus Christ the Bridegroom.

"That's amazing, Mrs. Clark."

"Call me Mama Clark," she smiled. "That's what everyone calls me." Her face glowing, she went on to describe a succession of Christmas trees, dating back many years.

"It's different every Christmas," she told me, raising her voice a little to be heard over the din. "Every year I decorate my tree with a different emphasis—but always something that shows a facet of the Lord's life and ministry."

Now she really had my attention. Passing a small mountain of mashed potatoes down the table, I asked her to tell me more.

The year before she had done Jesus the Creator, her tall pine adorned with photographs of natural wonders hanging from bright ribbons. You could see the Grand Canyon, Yellowstone Falls, and the Rocky Mountains, along with pictures of wildlife—deer and elk and mountain lions and bighorn sheep. Walking around her tree was like spending a day at "Mama Clark's Wild Kingdom." But all the glory went to Jesus, for "by him all things were created: things in heaven and on earth, visible and invisible...all things were created by him and for him" (Colossians 1:16).

Another year she featured Jesus the Teacher, festooning her large tree with pencils, tiny writing tablets, colored erasers, a little school bus, glittered report cards, miniature rulers, and a scattering of ABCs. In previous years her tree declared Jesus the Miracle Worker, Jesus the Savior, Jesus the Missionary, and Jesus the Intercessor.

With each passing year, she showcases a new aspect of the Lord's life and character for all to see. And many, many people *do* see. Mama Clark sends out invitations to an ever-widening circle; folks come from miles around, family by family, setting appointments to see her tree. As each family enters her home, Mama Clark seats them around the tree and serves cookies (baked in theme-appropriate shapes), coffee, and milk. Before the family leaves, she prays over each one that whatever facet of Christ's life was represented that year would be true in their lives all year long.

Before each of the families leaves Mama Clark's home, she asks them to sign a guest book. That guest book becomes Mama Clark's prayer list for the following year.

What a ministry this grandmother has! The passion of her life is to exalt the name of Jesus. She spends all year preparing for Christmas and praying for those who have crossed her threshold.

As we said our good-byes, I thought about asking if she ever worried about running out of "themes" each Christmas. But I think I know what her answer would have been. She would certainly run out of years before she ran out of ways to honor Jesus Christ. The important thing is to use the years you have.

And Mama Clark is doing just that.

How Can We Remember Him?

I felt a little uncomfortable as I pushed back from the table that day—and it wasn't because of the pumpkin pie. How am I proclaiming the Lord Jesus to my neighbors?

After I left Mama Clark that day, I almost found myself wishing my boys were small again so we could decorate our tree like she did. (Now I'll have to wait patiently until our baby granddaughter, Liesl Kate, is old enough to help me.)

Even if we didn't have the time or energy to change the theme every year, Joyce and I could find or make one special ornament for each Christmas…one ornament to remind us of the ways He has loved us. Then we could ask the children to search the tree to see if they could find that new ornament.

And finding it, we could sit down by the tree and talk about our Lord and all He means to us.

What kinds of ornaments? Mama Clark could decorate circles around me with one hand tied behind her back. But as I thought about it, I came up with just a few.

A little fishing boat could prompt us to remember how He taught the pressing crowds from near the shore…how He fell asleep in the boat after a long day of teaching, then stood up to still a fierce storm with a single command…how He told Peter when and where to cast his net for the biggest catch the big fisherman had ever seen.

A tiny wooden mallet might prod us to recall how He labored at Joseph's side in the carpenter's shop, a young man who loved His parents, loved His life, and lived in purity and obedience, quietly busy until the Spirit said, "It's time." Then, turning His face toward Jerusalem, He set down His carpenter's tools, never to pick them up again.

A sparkling star might represent the witness of the heavens to His coming…and remind us that He calls Himself the Bright Morning Star. Looking at that one little star on a tree, we could close our eyes and think of how it will be in heaven, when the Son of God will shine with pure, timeless radiance through the eternal morning. We won't need flashlights or night-lights—or even Christmas lights—in that new home. He Himself will be all the light we ever need, and it will never be dark again.

A tiny gold crown might call to mind His kingly splendor and remind us how the One called Faithful and True will ride through heaven's open door on a great white horse. "His eyes are like blazing fire, and on his head are many crowns.... On his robe and on his thigh he has this name written: KING OF KINGS AND LORD OF LORDS" (Revelation 19:12,16). As brothers and sisters of this mighty King, we will rule and reign with Him for a thousand years on earth—and then forevermore.

But not all the ornaments would be pretty.

A bit of *simple, homespun cloth* might remind us of His poverty—that the only thing He owned were the clothes on His back. And we would remember how the soldiers tore that clothing from His body, then cast lots for His undergarment.

A small, sharpened spike could help us remember that His hands and feet were nailed to rough timbers—to pay a ransom for our freedom that we could never pay.

A miniature circle of thorns would move us to think about the sort of crown our world thought appropriate for His brow. It might kindle a desire in our hearts to honor the One who was rejected and mocked and humbled, so that you and I might experience life.

Those are some of the ornaments that might decorate my Christmas tree in years to come. There are probably as many ideas for ornaments as there are people.

But in all our contemplations of decorations, lights, and

exterior adornments, we need to remember just what it is we celebrate. If we become preoccupied with externals and appearances, neglecting a heart of love, we have not honored God's greatest Gift. In fact, to our shame, we may even turn seeking men and women away from Him. I will never forget the time I did just that.

Too Busy to Give

A couple of years ago I sat at my gate at LAX, working feverishly on a Christmas sermon. Sometimes you can work for hours on a message or writing project, and it's like trying to ignite wet wood in a campfire. This time, however, the ideas caught fire. With my Bible open in my lap, I flipped pages and scribbled notes on a yellow pad. I could hardly write fast enough.

Out of the corner of my eye, I saw a man walk up to the seat next to me and set down two pencils with a note attached. Again and again he walked over to someone else and did the same thing. Two pencils and a note. I didn't take time to read the note. I'd seen this sort of thing before and knew basically what it said: "I'm deaf and dumb. I have no way to support my family. I have three kids. Would you give me some money for the pencils?"

Not only did I not read the note, I didn't even acknowledge him; I didn't look up or make eye contact. After a few minutes, the young man circled around again (as they always do). He came up to me, stopped for a moment, picked up his two pencils, and walked away. I breathed a little sigh of relief and went back to my sermon.

Then I caught something else out of the corner of my eye. Straight across from me was a young woman—maybe twenty to twenty-five years old. I sensed her staring at me.

The young man hadn't been away for more than a few seconds before she got up, walked over, and sat down right beside me. *Now what?* She looked right at me, her face hard and angry.

"Why didn't you give him any money?" she demanded.

"Well, uh," I stammered, "I think, uh…" She bored in on me.

"I saw you sitting there with your Bible, and I saw some other people give him a little money. But you didn't. You didn't even look at him. I suppose you're a preacher?"

I nodded.

"*That's* no great surprise," she said, her voice bitter. "That's the way most of you are. You preach it, but you don't live it. It's the same way with the people in your church, isn't it? They dress up on Sunday and smile and carry their Bibles. Well, I'll tell you something, I wouldn't go to church in a million worlds. *Why didn't you give him some money?* Do you have any money? Do you have a dollar? Do you have fifty cents? (She was merciless.) Couldn't you give him anything? Couldn't you at least *look* at the man. He can't hear. He can't speak. Nothing. And you—you just let him walk away."

I tried to speak with her, but my words seemed lame. Finally, they announced our flight. Sick at heart, I got up, closed my Bible, and walked to the plane.

We get so busy, so intense this time of year. Sitting there in that airport, I was probably working on a message about God's indescribable Gift. I was thumbing choice passages about that night long ago when a mighty choir of angels pierced the darkness with their song and the light of heaven came pouring through a great tear in the fabric of time and space. It was probably something eloquent. Something that would touch people's hearts. But I was so concerned about my message that I couldn't see a needy man standing right in front of me.

We've all been there. We've all found ourselves caught up in the trappings and wrappings of Christmas, singing carols with eyes half-closed. And then we realize we've closed our eyes to needs and hurts and longings right under our noses!

God, however, is gracious and forgiving. Just because we failed last Christmas (or the one before) doesn't mean we won't have a chance *this* year to let love break through.

Not long ago, I was once again sitting in an airport—this time in Portland—working on a sermon. Out of the corner of my eye, I saw a young man walk over to me and set down two pens with a little note. Then he walked around and distributed the pens to others—the same thing. He was deaf, unable to speak, and he needed money.

As he walked back to me, I was ready. I looked up. I

smiled. I mouthed the words "Jesus loves you" and gave him the few dollars I had in my wallet. And I praised my God for another opportunity to show forth His love!

That's the way love is. It finds a way.

Just as it did at Bethlehem.

CHAPTER TWO

Love Found a Way...
to Save Us

You are to give him the name Jesus,
because he will save his people from their sins.

MATTHEW 1:21

Grandpa walked into the family room and found his little grandson, Jeffy, standing up in his playpen, crying.

He looked so pitiful, standing there in his little baseball T-shirt and diaper. His face was red and tear-stained from crying. When Jeffy saw his grandpa, his face lit up in a way that smote the old man's heart. He immediately reached up his chubby little hands in supplication.

"Out Papa, *out!*"

What grandpa could resist such a plea? Not this one! He walked over to the playpen and reached down to lift his little buddy out of captivity and distress.

Just then, however, Law and Order stepped into the room.

Jeffy's mother walked out of the kitchen with a dishtowel in her hand and spoke sternly. "*No,* Jeffy! You are being

17

punished. You have to stay in bed! Leave him right there, Dad."

Oh fine. *Now* what's a grandpa to do? His grandson's tears and reaching little hands tugged mightily at his heart—but he didn't want to interfere with a mother's discipline either.

He couldn't stand staying in the same room with the boy, reading his newspaper and pretending to be aloof. Nor could he turn around and walk out the door without feeling like a betrayer to his little pal. What could he do?

Love found a way.

Since Grandpa couldn't take Jeffy *out* of the playpen, he climbed *in* with him. "If you're in the playpen, Buddy, I'm in the playpen. What's your sentence? How long are you in for?" And finding a big, jolly grandpa suddenly filling his little prison cell, the little boy found comfort even in his captivity.

Eyes Too Pure

What Jeffy's Grandpa did is a picture of what Jesus did for us at Christmas. As much as God would like to have picked us up and drawn us close, because of His holiness, He could not.

As the prophet wrote, "Your eyes are too pure to look on evil; you cannot tolerate wrong" (Habakkuk 1:13). David writes: "You are not a God who takes pleasure in evil; *with you the wicked cannot dwell*" (Psalm 5:4, emphasis added). Another translation says, "Those who do what is wrong can't live where you are" (NIrV). In other words, evil has no home with God. Evil could never stay with Him, lodge with Him, be near to Him.

Isaiah captures our situation with these words:

> But your sins have separated you from your God.
> They have caused him to turn his face away
> from you. (Isaiah 59:2, NIrV)

And yet He loved us. John 3:16 says "God so *loved* the world."

He had compassion for us. He yearned for us. What was a holy God to do?

Because His love was so great, He sent His Son to "climb into the playpen" with us. We couldn't live with God, so God came to live with us. Jesus couldn't bring us to His house, so He came to our house. John writes, "The Word became flesh and made his dwelling among us. We have seen his glory, the glory of the One and Only, who came from the Father, full of grace and truth" (John 1:14).

Jesus pitched His tent among us. The joy of Christmas is knowing that it was the only way He could bring us home to Himself. The only way was for Him to become a man and then come and save us.

What It Took

Whenever I drive to the east side of Portland over the Marquam Bridge, I'm reminded just a little of what it took for God to save us. On the upper deck of that two-decker freeway spanning the wide Willamette River, you can sometimes catch a glimpse of an exit that drops off into empty space.

When the bridge was built back in the mid-1960s, it was designed to accommodate an east-running freeway still on the drawing boards, which was to be known as the Mount Hood Freeway. But the freeway was never built. Even though land on the east side had been purchased and cleared for its path, Oregon voters opted for a light rail line instead, and plans for the highway were scrapped.

Even though there is no Mount Hood Freeway, you can certainly see Mount Hood from the top deck of the Marquam Bridge. On clear days it looms on the eastern horizon—a symmetrical, snow-capped beauty. And if you look carefully, you can see how the bridge was built to accommodate a freeway lane veering off to the southeast. It juts out just a bit from the bridge structure, then is cut off as though sliced by a giant knife.

The "exit," permanently blocked, now goes no-where…except into the waters of the Willamette far below. You can see Mount Hood in all its beauty, glistening like a jewel in the distance. In the evenings, the setting sun clothes it with a mantle of pink and gold. But you could never, never reach the high slopes of that mighty peak via the Mount Hood Freeway, because…the freeway doesn't exist.

That's a picture of man's relationship with God. We might understand that there is a God and even yearn to reach Him across an impossible distance. We might recognize His power and glory, His majesty and goodness, and desire with all our hearts to know Him and be with Him. But the distance is too great. The gulf is too wide.

I wonder if Beatle George Harrison didn't sense this insurmountable chasm. I remember a Harrison tune that dominated the airwaves for a time back in the 1970s. In the song he spoke about really wanting to see and be with "my sweet Lord." But then the singer seemed to sigh, shrug his shoulders, and add: "But it takes so long…"

Harrison looked all over the world for a relationship with God, and I don't know that he ever found it. But the words of his song always sounded so wistful and sad to me…as though this young man with so much money and so much fame yearned after the living God but couldn't reach Him.

None of us can reach Him. None of us can see Him or be near Him. Not on our own! Wealth or celebrity or great talent won't help us at all. The relationship that existed back in Eden was broken, the road shattered. The exit ramp to God's presence was cut off and ended in empty space.

God had to make a way where there was no way. And He had to build the road from the heaven side of the gulf, because we could do nothing to build from our side. Only He could have done it.

I could never have found a way. You could never have found a way. Because there was no way…until God made one. The writer of Hebrews called it "a new and living way opened for us" (Hebrews 10:20). Peter bluntly warned his audience not to search for any other road: "Salvation is found in no one else," he said, "for there is no other name under heaven given to men by which we must be saved" (Acts 4:12).

A Midnight Groundbreaking

Some freeway projects begin with a "groundbreaking" cere-mony where public officials who haven't held a shovel for thirty years get to put on hard hats, pose for pictures, and dig about a cup full of dirt to launch construction.

The new and living way, the way back to reconciliation with a righteous God, didn't begin with public officials wear-ing ties and hard hats, smiling into TV cameras. It didn't begin with ribbon cutting or phony handshakes or speeches in front of the media.

As a matter of fact, construction began in the depths of night, in a little stable behind a busy hotel. It began with the moans of a Jewish girl in the pangs of birth…and the tiny cry of an infant.

That night the ground was broken. A highway that would be traveled by millions, a highway stretching through time and space into the golden lands of heaven began that night. Mary cradled the Way, the Truth, and the Life in her arms, a few shepherds looked on with wondering eyes, and Joseph whispered, "Emmanuel…*God with us!*"

Even the name they gave Him pointed to His unique place in God's scheme of things. The name Jesus is *Yeshua* in Hebrew, often translated as "Joshua." It means, "God saves." In a very real sense, you could translate that name *God to the rescue.* The baby Mary carried in her womb was not only God's Son, but the world's Savior. He came as Jesus…"God to the rescue."

Jesus was a common name in those days, just as Mike or John or Jennifer would be today. Many boys were named Jesus. But this Jesus wasn't like the others; this Jesus would truly live up to His name. His name was not only a declaration of the fact that "Yahweh saves," this was God Himself doing the saving! He would save His people.

So here in the original Christmas we see the shadow of the cross, the beginning of this journey toward Good Friday and Easter. It's all one story. The reason Jesus came as a baby was to die as a man on a cross. To make a way where there was no way.

God to the Rescue

When we look into the manger, we see a Savior there, just as godly Simeon did when he spotted the baby Jesus in the temple courts just after the Lord's birth:

> Simeon took him in his arms and praised God, saying: "Sovereign Lord, as you have promised, you now dismiss your servant in peace. For my eyes have seen your salvation, which you have prepared in the sight of all people, a light for revelation to the Gentiles and for glory to your people Israel." (Luke 2:28-32)

And, oh, how rich this "salvation" was in Simeon's eyes! It gave him "peace," it showered him with "light," and it set his mind on "glory"!

Have you ever stopped to think about how rich is our salvation in Jesus? Whole libraries could be written to expound the subject, but let's mention just three of these riches:

1. He Saved Us from Our Sins

First John 3:5 tells us clearly: "But you know that he appeared so that he might take away our sins. And in him is no sin."

One of the reasons Christ came was so that you and I

wouldn't have to carry around the weight and grief of our sin all of our lives. He came to release me from the sin of my past, my shame, and the chains of sins and habits and addictions that keep me hurting people and hurting myself over and over again. He wanted me to know the joy and blessing of being released from that crushing load of sin.

I richly deserved God's judgment, but Jesus took my judgment upon His own shoulders. Simeon saw all that in the infant he held that first Christmas.

2. He Came to Destroy the Works of the Enemy
John wrote: "The reason the Son of God appeared was to destroy the devil's work" (1 John 3:8).

Jesus came to destroy, or undo, the works of the enemy. Because He came, there can now be a different outlook for my life. Satan's desire for me will not be accomplished!

Martin Luther wrote:

> The prince of darkness grim
> We tremble not for him,
> His rage we can endure,
> For lo, his doom is sure,
> One little word shall fell him!

And what is that word? The Word is Jesus.
Yeshua.
God to the rescue.

God did not want Satan, the enemy of my soul, to destroy, thwart, or abort His purpose, plans, and desires for me. So He sent His Son, not only to release me from my sin, but also to rescue me from this designed, orchestrated plan of the enemy to destroy my life, home, and family.

3. He Came to Reveal the Father

> This is how God showed his love among us: He sent his one and only Son into the world that we might live through him. (1 John 4:9)

Jesus came to let us know how much God loves us. I rejoice in the fact that Jesus came to make sure we really knew how God feels toward you and me. When you read the Gospels, every time you see the Lord reaching out to help, bless, heal, comfort, or deliver someone, you're seeing the very heart of God. God loves people. His heart is deeply concerned for men and women and children.

Arthur John Gossip, a pastor from a bygone age, wrote:

> The wonderful thing about Christ is that as people looked at Him, followed Him, and watched Him, it became apparent to them that this is what God must be like. They concluded that if there is a God at all, then He must have Christ's eyes, Christ's ways, Christ's ever-helpful

hands, Christ's character.... Stand upon Calvary and know that if today He loves like that, He always loves like that. Even when our hearts become hot and suspicious of Him or soured and bad-tempered toward Him for His ordering of our lives and crossing our wishes, He still loves us. To be God means always to stoop lower by far than any man could stoop, to bear what never a human heart would dream of bearing, to give Oneself with an abandon of unselfishness that leaves us staring in slack-jawed wonder. His love is a hugeness beyond all human reckoning. It is an everlasting Calvary.[1]

The Greatest Christmas Gift

God so loved that He *gave*. That's what happened at Christmas. It was a gift of love. Some say the tradition of gift-giving started with the gifts of the magi. But the truth is, gift-giving began when God gave Jesus, His Son, to save us.

I'd like to wrap up this chapter by recalling what an old preacher of the gospel said more than a century ago. The Reverend Edward Payson told his flock,

> There is more of God—more of His essential glory displayed in bringing one sinner to

repentance and forgiving his sins—than in all the wonders of creation. In this great work, men and angels may see the very heart of God.

From this work, angels themselves have probably learned more of God's moral character than they had ever been able to discover before. They knew that God was wise and powerful, for they had seen Him create a world. They knew He was good, for He had made them perfectly holy and happy. They knew He was just, for they had seen Him cast down their own rebellious associates from heaven to hell for their sins. But until they saw Him give repentance and forgiveness of sins through Christ, they did not know that He was merciful; they did not know that He could pardon a sinner.

And O! what an hour it was in heaven when this great truth was first made known, when the first repentant sinner was pardoned! Then a new song burst from the mouths of heaven's angels. And with indescribable emotions of wonder, love, and praise, they began to sing, their voices swelled to a higher pitch, and they experienced joys unfelt before.

O how did the joyful sounds, "His love endures forever," spread from choir to choir, echo through the high arches of heaven, and thrill through every enraptured angelic breast! And how they cried, with one voice, "Glory to God in the highest, and on earth peace to men on whom his favor rests"![2]

CHAPTER THREE

Love Found a Way...
to Help Us

"The virgin will be with child and will give birth
to a son, and they will call him Immanuel"—
which means, "God with us."

MATTHEW 1:23

Though only a young girl at the time, Judy Rogers remembers the year her father was laid off work. Family finances, already lean, became leaner still.

Christmas was coming, and for months Judy's father had been promising his wife a new dishwasher. That good woman was still recuperating from breast cancer surgery, making it painful to do some of the usual household chores.

But a *dishwasher?* It seemed impossible—or at least wildly improbable. Where would the money come from? They were barely able to make payments on their medical bills and still make the mortgage as it was. In addition, the house had old wiring and plumbing. Even if they were somehow able to scrape together the money to buy such a luxury, it could never be installed without major remodeling.

The obstacles! Another man might have shrunk before such barriers. But Judy's dad had made a promise, and he was a man who took his promises seriously. Somehow, he would find a way to do it.

Judy remembered how her father hated the thought of even touching dirty dishes. He was a man's man, and in the world he'd grown up in, men stayed out of the kitchen (excepting an occasional foray to raid the refrigerator). He had said on several occasions he would rather tackle almost any hard outdoor chore he could think of than face a stack of dirty dinnerware in the sink.

But then again...how could he let his wife do work that was hurting her? Of course, she always minimized the discomfort. Said it was nothing. She'd be fine, she said. She looked fine too—to most everyone else—and held on to the smile so treasured by her friends.

But her husband knew better. He'd heard the sighs—and those times when a stab of pain made her catch her breath. He saw the shadows of weariness under her eyes.

He *had* to find a way. Judy remembered him brooding in the days leading up to Christmas—staring out the window at the gray winter skies, his hands in his pockets. He was always a capable, resourceful man, but this mountain seemed too large for even him to climb.

Christmas Day came with no mysterious deliveries. No large box appeared next to the tree. There were no visits from the plumber or the electrician. There was nothing but a few carefully wrapped gifts under the tree.

And a small envelope.

Within the envelope was a note—a handwritten letter from Dad. The note read:

> For one year, I will wash all of the dirty dishes in this household…every one.

And he did.

Who Else But God

I wept when I first heard this story, because it reminds me so much of what God has done for us. He saw our predicament. He knows our weaknesses and failings. He has heard our sighs, seen our tears, and weighed burdens in our heart that no one else sees or knows.

But how could a holy God redeem and help sinful man? To the angels in heaven looking on, it must have seemed so impossible. But angels know, better than most, that this is a God who takes His promises very, very seriously. If He committed Himself to help, He certainly would.

And He did. But not in a way any man or angel or demon might have expected. He did it by giving Himself. He did it by rolling up His sleeves and stepping personally into

His own fallen creation. In the face of impossible obstacles, Love found a way.

Christmas speaks strongly of God's personal gift to us all.

The angel—his mind swept with wonder and awe—must have grappled with the implications when he told the shepherds:

> For unto you is born this day in the city
> of David a Saviour, which is Christ the Lord.
> (Luke 2:11, KJV)

FOR UNTO YOU... It's *personal.* Have you let that thought weave its way through your yuletide meditations and memories? He designed Christmas with *you* in mind. He came personally for *you.* The Savior was born "unto *you.*" I find myself realizing how special Christmas is when I contemplate the fact that—somehow, in some incomprehensible way—He was thinking about me when He came. What He did, He did for me. What He gave, He gave for me. What He suffered, He suffered for my sake. And He held nothing back.

IS BORN... It's *miraculous,* because the Holy Spirit—not you—has conceived what, to us, was inconceivable. Christmas isn't something conjured up by man for the purpose of self-congratulation; it celebrates the moment when God stepped out of heaven's radiance into the cold stream of time and space. You and I couldn't lift a finger to redeem ourselves, so He made that long journey to be our help.

THIS DAY… It's *immediate,* because God wants life to happen in you today, this moment. There is no need to wait any longer. God wants to birth something in you today.

He came to help us. He's promised to give us guidance, good counsel, and daily provision. The help He provides is something no one else can provide. In the classic movie *It's a Wonderful Life,* George Bailey had Clarence the Angel to help. But in this life, we need more than Clarence, as wonderful as he may have been. We need the help of God Himself.

If you let the Christmas season pass without realizing that He was born for you, lived and walked this earth for you, died and rose again for you, you've missed it. You might as well have slept through the whole month of December.

It Really Happened

On one of my trips to Israel, I remember sitting by myself on a stone bench at the Garden Tomb. Our group had just shared a little communion service, and the rest of them had wandered off along the pathways to look at other things. But I felt like staying. I wanted to just sit quietly for a while beside the tomb.

The growing heat of that Middle-Eastern morning sun made me move a bit into the shade. Closing my eyes, I could smell the fragrance of the flowers and hear the rustling of the leaves, rippled by a passing breeze. And suddenly, in that moment, the truth—the *reality*—of His coming hit me as it had never hit me before. While I had spoken and taught countless times about our Lord's death on the cross and His resurrection, the wonder of it all just gripped me that quiet morning in the garden.

In that place, in that moment, it all became so fresh and personal to me. The Son of God had *really* left heaven! He came clothed in human flesh, born as a little baby in a humble stable not over six miles from where I sat at that very moment. And just yards away, the mighty Second Person of the Holy Trinity became the Lamb of God and died on a Roman cross. It happened! He was buried in a tomb—perhaps *this* tomb—and then came forth from the grave in victory and glory and great power.

Suddenly the words of Galatians 4:4-5 took on even brighter colors than I had known before:

> But when the time had fully come, God sent his
> Son, born of a woman, born under law, to
> redeem those under law, that we might receive
> the full rights of sons.

And I thought: *If this story had stopped before Calvary, I would still be lost in my sins. I would still be on my own in life, grabbing for a little sweetness or excitement wherever I could find it, before death claimed me and sent me into eternal darkness.*

But the story did not stop before Calvary. The Author just kept on writing. And He did it for me. He did it for you.

On that same trip, we toured Bethlehem and saw the shepherds' fields. We sat on the Mount of Beatitudes and looked out across the Sea of Galilee. We stood on the excavated steps of Herod's temple in Jerusalem, where Jesus most certainly had stood a number of times. If His story had stopped at Bethlehem, it would have been nothing more than a nice, sweet, religious homily—poignant and a little sad. If the story had ended at Galilee or in the temple, it might have been an inspiring account—but it would have been no help to me at all. I didn't need inspiration, I needed *salvation.*

But—praise His name!—Jesus didn't stay in Bethlehem. He didn't stay by the blue waters of Galilee, or in the quiet carpenter's shop in Nazareth, or on the steps of the stately temple. He stayed obedient all the way to the cross. As Galatians 3:13 tells us, "Christ redeemed us from the curse of the law by becoming a curse for us." And because He did that for me, I have an unspeakably great source of encouragement, blessing, and hope.

I am *helped.* I can sing with David,

> God is our refuge and strength,
>   an ever-present help in trouble. (Psalm 46:1)

Surely God is my help;
> the Lord is the one who sustains me. (Psalm 54:4)

Because you are my help,
> I sing in the shadow of your wings. (Psalm 63:7)

What lengths He went to help! What obstacles heaven had to overcome! How awesome that love found a way!

When the Storm Hits

In Matthew 14, the gospel writer gives us a wonderful picture of how unwilling the Lord was for His story to stop at Bethlehem. Matthew tells how the Lord Jesus sent His disciples across the Sea of Galilee after a busy day of ministry while He stayed behind to pray. As daylight faded, a storm came up, sweeping down the mountain, churning the sea into a dangerous caldron.

Mark adds the detail that when the boat was in the middle of the lake, Jesus "saw the disciples straining at the oars, because the wind was against them" (Mark 6:48).

The word Mark used for "straining" speaks of hard toil and comes from a word meaning "to torture." There was great pain and torment of body and soul that night as those men rowed for their lives "against the wind." The text literally says the wind was "contrary to them." It was antagonistic to their purpose, fighting them for every inch.

And Jesus saw them.

In fact, He had watched their whole struggle from the time the first cloud shadowed the setting sun and the first ominous breeze blew across their bow. He had been praying for them. And now He was about to meet them at their point of need. The disciples must have despaired, imagining that they were out of sight from their Lord in the darkness and the storm. They thought He couldn't hear their cries. But He saw and He heard. As David wrote:

> In my alarm I said,
>> "I am cut off from your sight!"
> Yet you heard my cry for mercy
>> when I called to you for help. (Psalm 31:22)

And then He came to them. He walked right into the night, into the teeth of the wind, into the fury of the storm.

Does that move you as it moves me? This isn't a God who watches from a safe distance. This is no sleepy, apathetic God who idly observes the suffering of His creatures like so many microscopic entities on a glass slide. This is God With Us. Emmanuel comes down from the mountain and steps onto the dark, foaming sea. He moves near. He steps into our storm.

> About the fourth watch of the night he went out
> to them, walking on the lake. He was about to
> pass by them, but when they saw him walking on

the lake, they thought he was a ghost. They cried out, because they all saw him and were terrified.

Immediately he spoke to them and said, "Take courage! It is I. Don't be afraid." Then he climbed into the boat with them, and the wind died down. (Mark 6:48-51)

The wind had been against them. Contrary to them. Antagonistic to their efforts and goals and desires. Isn't that a picture of life? Maybe circumstances have been "contrary" to you in recent days. Maybe you feel as though you've been walking against the wind or rowing until your heart breaks, but making no progress at all.

What can keep you, and what keeps me, is the knowledge that God watches it all. Jesus sees everything. He sees our struggles. He sees us strain at the oars. He knows when the wind is against us. And this very day He prays and intercedes for us at the right hand of the Father. But He doesn't just watch. He comes to us—at the right time. It may not be the time we want, but it is at the right time. He steps into our circumstances to help us.

This is a Savior who will pay any price. He'll walk on water. He'll shoulder His way into the storms of hell. He'll endure the righteous wrath of His Father. And He'll show up wherever life leads you. He will not be indifferent to your challenges and difficulties, your perplexities and hardships.

In His love, He will find a way to help.

When No One Else Can Help

You and I are competent, reasonably intelligent people, accustomed to helping ourselves whenever we can. But life has a way of placing us into positions where we are powerless to make any difference. People will often say, "Well, somehow it always works out." But now we're talking about things that aren't going to work out. Storms that can't be calmed. Walls that can't be scaled. Problems that defy man-made solutions and baffle our best attempts to understand. No one else can help you. You can't help yourself. You strain at the oars until your hands bleed, but you're heading into a contrary wind, you're taking on water, and you're getting nowhere at all.

If you find yourself in that kind of agonizing predicament, I urge you to look to the same source that dazzled Mary shortly after she discovered she had been chosen to bear the Savior of the world. At the end of what has come to be known as The Magnificat, she exclaimed to her cousin Elizabeth that God "has helped his servant Israel, remembering to be merciful to Abraham and his descendants forever, even as he said to our fathers" (Luke 1:54-55).

So look up, friend. The Lord God is walking right into your storm. Don't let Him walk on by. Receive Him into your boat and wait for Him to speak to the wind and the waves.

Christmas reminds us that there's no help like His.

CHAPTER FOUR

Love Found a Way...
to Enable Us

His mother Mary was pledged to be married to Joseph,
but before they came together, she was found
to be with child through the Holy Spirit.

MATTHEW 1:18

Mary, informed she would be with child, asked the angel Gabriel a most logical question.

"How can this be?"

What the angel had told her, besides being startling, was physically impossible. Mary knew a virgin couldn't possibly conceive a child—and that's what she was.

Gabriel replied to her, in so many words, "Don't worry. God will enable you to do this." And then (if angels are capable of it), I can imagine a twinkle in his eye as he added, "He will enable you to do something and be something you could never have thought possible."

No woman in all of history had faced a situation like Mary's. We might say something similar about our lives. No one has been in your precise set of circumstances, facing

43

exactly what you face as you read these words. As the old spiritual put it, "Nobody knows the trials I've seen...." Yet all of us know what it means to struggle with weaknesses, inadequacies, and unyielding obstacles. We look at certain situations and relationships and despair of ever seeing change.

When I first began preaching at what was then a little mission church in Beaverton, Oregon, I would sometimes feel so disappointed in my own preaching that I left the pulpit feeling physically sick. I remember kneeling by myself in a little room off the sanctuary, my face pressed into the cold metal of a folding chair. "Why do You have me here?" I asked the Lord. "Why did You call me to this place? What did these good people do to deserve such a poor excuse for a pastor? I can't do this, Lord! It's too much for me."

It turned out I was right. For over twenty-five years now, it *has* been too much for me. But it hasn't been too much for Him. Love finds a way to enable us.

A Two-Part Answer

Life has a way of exposing our weaknesses. We are weak vessels. Jars of clay. Yet God leads us to difficult tasks so that we might turn to Him. It is the power of God that enables us.

To Mary's question, "How can this be?" Gabriel offered a two-part answer. First, he reminded her that this would be the work of the Holy Spirit within her, not something of her own strength or doing. And second, he pointed her to another miracle near at hand—right in Mary's own family.

1. Depend on the Empowering of the Holy Spirit

> The angel answered, "The Holy Spirit will come upon you, and the power of the Most High will overshadow you. So the holy one to be born will be called the Son of God." (Luke 1:35)

Have you ever found yourself painted into one of those "impossible corners" in your life? The tasks before you seem crushing. The obstacles insurmountable. The complexities overwhelming. You can't seem to make any forward progress, but know you can't turn back. You don't know what to do or where to turn.

What I love so much about Scripture is the way it repeatedly shows us that we are not alone in those feelings. Others have "been there" before us, in corners just as tight, in circumstances every bit as demanding. And the pages of the Bible show us how the Lord has been pleased to help and deliver time after time. Listen, for instance, to Paul's candid confession to the Corinthians:

> We do not want you to be uninformed, brothers, about the hardships we suffered in the province of Asia. We were under great pressure, far beyond

our ability to endure, so that we despaired even of
life. Indeed, in our hearts we felt the sentence of
death. (2 Corinthians 1:8-9)

Does any of that sound familiar? Have you been in such
a place? Have you tasted the "great pressure"? Have you felt
that inability to endure even one more day? Have you felt
despair creeping up—like fog through the floorboards—to
wrap its fingers around your heart? That's what the great
apostle Paul experienced. But listen to what he learned
through that process:

But this happened that we might not rely on ourselves but on God, who raises the dead. (verse 9)

The Living Bible captures Paul's emotions like this: "We
were really crushed and overwhelmed, and feared we would
never live through it. We...saw how powerless we were to
help ourselves; but that was good, for then we put everything
into the hands of God, who alone could save us."

When you are crushed and overwhelmed, when the
problem seems so much bigger than you and you feel powerless to make a difference, there is One who will enable you
to go on. There is One who will put His shoulder under your
load, if you will cast your cares upon Him.

Mary asked, "How will this be?" And Gabriel replied,
"The Holy Spirit will come upon you." And then he added

what must be one of the most encouraging statements in all of Scripture: "For *nothing* is impossible with God" (Luke 1:34-37, emphasis added).

It's just the same for you and me. When we find ourselves overmatched by our circumstances, overwhelmed by responsibilities, and overburdened by problems beyond our ability to handle, we must cry out to God and lean on the enabling of the One who dwells within us.

It is one of the reasons Jesus came. He looked around and saw men and women staggering under the load of worries and cares and tasks, and His heart was moved within Him. He said, "Come to me, all you who are weary and burdened, and I will give you rest" (Matthew 11:28).

Paul faced the same situation once again a bit later in the book of 2 Corinthians. He confessed a physical "thorn in the flesh" that grieved and tormented him. Three times he pleaded with the Lord for release from that affliction, and three times He was given this answer: "My grace is all you need. My power is strongest when you are weak" (12:9, NIrV).

In other words, "My strength and My power are at work in the midst of your weakness, in the midst of your impossible situations, in the midst of those times when you wonder, *What in the world am I going to do?*"

You and I limit God's work in our lives by not allowing Him to enable us! We don't give Him our burdens because they seem so impossible to us. We say, "What's the use? I want God to work in me, but my life is a mess and God could never enable *me*."

That's not what Mary did. Even though she couldn't begin to understand how God was about to accomplish what He said He would accomplish in her, she simply bowed her head and submitted to God's plan. "'I am the Lord's servant,' Mary answered. 'May it be to me as you have said'" (Luke 1:38). Centuries earlier, in another moment of great distress and perplexity, the prophet Jeremiah bowed his head in a similar way and said:

> Ah, Sovereign LORD, you have made the
> heavens and the earth by your great power
> and outstretched arm. Nothing is too hard
> for you. (Jeremiah 32:17)

2. Witness His Work in Those Around You
After the angel reminded Mary that the power of the Holy Spirit would do the impossible within her, He encouraged her to pack her pajamas and toothbrush and take a little trip.

> Even Elizabeth your relative is going to have a
> child in her old age, and she who was said to be
> barren is in her sixth month. (Luke 1:36)

If you feel powerless, if you struggle believing that God could enable you to do something extraordinary—or do an extraordinary work in you—*look around and see what He's done for others!* That's exactly what Mary did. She immediately took the angel's hint (always a good idea) and "got ready and hurried to a town in the hill country of Judea" (Luke 1:39).

Mary *ran* to Elizabeth. She made haste. Why did she hurry? Because Elizabeth was a living illustration that God, working within a woman's yielded life, could do the impossible. Zechariah was "well along in years," and Elizabeth "was barren." Yet now she was six months along!

Mary craved that living illustration of God's power and might. And when Elizabeth greeted Mary at the door, the older woman's stomach round with new life, Mary's heart must have sung with joy. Perhaps at that moment God whispered in her heart, "If I can work in her, My daughter, I can work in you."

Elizabeth's greeting certainly removed any lingering doubt: "Blessed are you among women, and blessed is the child you will bear!… Blessed is she who has believed that what the Lord has said to her will be accomplished!" (verses 42,45).

And then Mary burst into song! When she saw how God had worked in her relative's heart and how Elizabeth had been filled with the Holy Spirit, she, too, was filled with the Holy Spirit…and great joy!

Mary spoke of three specific blessings from the Lord. First, she spoke of the blessing of *peace*.

For the Mighty One has done great things for me—
holy is his name. (verse 49)

When God says He'll do something, He will do it. Mary must have had great confusion in her mind since her conversation with Gabriel. There were so many things she couldn't fit together. What would Joseph think? What would the neighbors say? What would the elders do? What would her family imagine?

Yet now her heart focuses on "the Mighty One"—who He is and what He has done. What the peace of God does is to piece things together. It takes all the broken, puzzling fragments in our mind and brings them together in His peace.

Second, she spoke of the blessing of *protection.*

He has brought down rulers from their thrones
but has lifted up the humble. (verse 52)

Mary sang of past deliverances of her fathers in the faith. No power can withstand God's might. God will remove any obstacle that rises to hinder His work. Nothing will get in the way. What God has set Himself to do, He will do.

Third, she spoke of the blessing of *power.*

He has helped his servant Israel,
remembering to be merciful

to Abraham and his descendants forever,
even as he said to our fathers. (verses 54-55)

Mary stood on the history and track record of God. No, she had never been in the frightening situation in which she found herself. But she recognized that God was still God, no matter what was happening in her life. This is a God who had done miracles before! He gave Abraham and Sarah a child in their old age. Life came forth from Sarah's dead womb, a miracle baby whose name meant "laughter." Mary encouraged herself by recalling God's mighty, miraculous works in the past. She reminded herself that she wasn't God's first project.

Mary might have said something like this to herself, as she walked the dusty miles to Zechariah and Elizabeth's home in the hills. "I'm just a young girl, and my mind is filled with questions and confusion. The best thing I can do right now is to rehearse in my mind the mighty things my God has done. Why shouldn't I believe He can do a mighty work in me?"

We can learn from Mary the value of declaring what God has done in our lives. God will use our words, our firsthand experience of His grace and power, to encourage others who struggle with fear or worry or discouragement.

I saw that take place in a moving way here at our church. I saw the lasting impact of a man who believed with all his heart that love would find a way.

The Gardener on His Knees

My friend Ben Castile was a man with holy determination. I presided at his funeral just yesterday. An elder of elders and one of the great men in my life, Ben was ninety years old when he stepped out of this world and into his Lord's embrace.

As people came up after the service to walk by the casket and say their good-byes, I noticed a young man coming forward, hand-in-hand with his little boy. After the funeral, I received an explanation from that young dad.

Terry Smith is on staff here at the church. He and his wife, Lisa, are a handsome couple with five beautiful children. But Austin, their youngest, was born with severe neurological damage. At his birth, doctors said he was legally blind and that his brain was severely damaged. They told Terry and Lisa that the boy should certainly be institutionalized. Terry had seen the EEG results himself and could see the spike marks, revealing serious abnormalities. I was there. I witnessed it too.

Gently but firmly, the doctors pressed their point. There was no hope for Austin ever to be normal.

The baby was in the ICU for three to four months. During those long weeks, Terry and Lisa sat with him every day. As Christmas drew near that year, Terry told me how he hovered by that little incubator and sang Christmas carols to his tiny, helpless son. One night after singing "Silent Night," Terry fell asleep, his head resting on the incubator.

In reality, there was nothing "silent" about that night. The circumstances seemed to scream out loud at this dear young couple. Everything was chaos, not "calm and bright."

Ben worked at the church too, as a landscaper. The two men would often open their lunchboxes and eat together. It was during one of those times that Terry poured out his heart, telling his older friend about Austin's current condition.

"The prognosis isn't good, Ben," Terry told him. "I don't know what's going to happen."

Ben was silent for a moment, then looked Terry in the eyes and said, "You just watch. He'll be the smartest boy in his class."

Ben Castile had been one of the state's top landscapers. When it came time to retire, he sold his business and offered his services to our church. He always seemed to be on his knees, working with the flowers and trees on our campus.

Ben used to say, "When I'm working with the plants and trees, it reminds me of how God so patiently works on me." Ben never gave up on the trees and shrubs committed to his charge. I would sometimes say, "That one's done for, Ben. Why waste your time? You may as well dig that thing up and get rid of it."

But he would smile, tip back his hat and say, "Give it a little more time, Pastor. It just needs some love and attention." And the next thing I knew, it would be flourishing. Ben never gave up on anything or anyone, reminding me of the words in 1 Corinthians 13:

> Love suffers long and is kind; love…bears all
> things, believes all things, hopes all things,
> endures all things.
>> Love never fails. (verses 4,7-8, NKJV)

During those first difficult months of Austin's life and through the intervening years, there never was a day that old Ben didn't pray for Terry and Lisa's boy. Already on his knees much of the day, tending the trees, shrubbery, and flowers, Ben used the kneeling time to keep Austin before the throne of heaven.

Terry and Lisa would bring all of their children to visit "Grandpa Ben" through the years, and Austin grew up knowing his life was tended by a very special gardener.

Just before Ben passed away, Terry and Lisa were thrilled to show him Austin's report card. He was now eight years old and at the top of his class in several subjects.

Ben smiled. He didn't say, "I told you so." He really didn't need to.

Love Never Gives Up

While Austin's motor skills still need help, he is no longer blind, and his EEG results are perfectly normal. (Terry has also seen those results.)

Austin knows his own history. He knows he had been very, very weak and has been getting better and stronger—

little by little, day by day—because of what the Lord has done. He attributes much of that to the determined prayers of Grandpa Ben, a man who refused to give up on trees, flowers…or little boys committed to his charge.

So it was that little Austin, on the day of the funeral, asked his dad to take him up to the casket. With tears in his eyes, he said good-bye to Grandpa Ben…the man who believed love would find a way.

And it did.

CHAPTER FIVE

Love Found a Way...
to Bring Us Joy

An angel of the Lord appeared to them,
and the glory of the Lord shone around them,
and they were terrified. But the angel said to them,
"Do not be afraid. I bring you good news
of great joy that will be for all the people."

LUKE 2:9-10

I know there's no such thing as "luck" in heaven, but…I can't help but think that the angel who delivered this message must have felt very, very privileged. Out of all the countless millions of angels, how did he get tapped for that job? Seniority? Did they draw a number? Take applications? Review résumés?

After all, it isn't every angel who gets to step into time and space, make a visible appearance on the earth, and deliver the best news this old planet had ever heard in its long, unhappy history. It isn't every angel who gets to herald the birth of the King of kings.

Did he say, "good news"?

Seems like something of an understatement, doesn't it? We talk about "good news" when Johnny gets a B on his report card or the dog has puppies or we sew up a reservation for our favorite camping spot at the state park.

"Good news"?

There has never been better news. The people living in darkness would see a great light. A *Savior* had been born, and He would save His people from their sins.

As Mary sang in her song of praise, "My soul glorifies the Lord and my spirit rejoices in God my Savior, for he has been mindful of the humble state of his servant" (Luke 1:46-48).

Joy in a Disappointing World

Of all seasons, Christmas is particularly a time of joy...but not for everyone. We live in a world where people endure many disappointments. Friends forget to write to you, call you back, or return your greeting. Associates may ignore your messages or spurn your invitations.

I remember visiting my mom during her stay in a senior care center. As I sat with her a number of times in the open common area, I couldn't help but notice an elderly woman make her way to her mailbox at least a couple of times a day.

But the box was always empty.

Mom told me that this lady did this every day, hoping she might hear from her family—but she never did.

But even more heartbreaking to me was something that

happened that evening. Sitting with my mom there in the common area, I watched as a number of these dear folks, many of them old and frail, began to gather. They were all dressed up in their Sunday-go-to-meetin' clothes, waiting for the guest choir to arrive and give a little concert of their favorite hymns and Christmas carols.

As we waited, a staff worker abruptly entered the room and wrote on the wipe-off board, in large block letters, "THE CHOIR HAD TO CANCEL." That was it. No explanation, no apology. Just a note on the board.

You could feel the letdown in that room. For a few minutes, everyone just sat there. Then, one by one, they filed out.

I wasn't feeling very charitable about a certain choir at that moment. Truthfully, I was angry. Why had they cancelled? Did they get a better offer? Was it for selfish reasons? I found myself hurting for these dear people who had only one thing to look forward to that Christmas, and that was the local church choir coming to sing for them.

But this is the kind of world we live in...a world where choirs cancel and leave old people disappointed, where you go to the mailbox and find nothing there. They say earth's atmosphere is composed of mostly nitrogen and oxygen. But sometimes it seems that a third major element in that gaseous mix is disappointment. It's as common as the air we breathe. You long for someone to say something and they don't. You hope for something to fulfill you and it doesn't. So often we go to bed with an ache in our hearts.

But God, in His love, finds a way to bring us joy. Joy in *Himself*, not dependent on circumstances. God finds a way to put hope into your mailbox. He never spurns an invitation. When we seek Him with our whole heart, we *find* Him! (The Bible guarantees it.) He comes to our parties. He answers our calls. He shows up early and lingers late. He is never thinking of something else or preoccupied when we pour out our hearts to Him. When Jesus makes an appointment, He always keeps it. He never forgets. He never stands you up, cancels out, or asks for a rain check. When we pin our hopes on Him, we are never disappointed. As the Lord tells us in the book of Isaiah, "Those who hope in me will not be disappointed" (Isaiah 49:23).

Isn't That Overdoing It?

Paul reminds us to "rejoice always."

But doesn't that seem like "overdoing it"? Doesn't that strike you as a little extreme?

It really isn't...after you think through some of the apostle's reasoning. Why *shouldn't* we rejoice always, when we truly begin to understand the height and depth and length and width of God's love for us? Paul wrote to his friends in Ephesus:

> I fall down on my knees and pray to the
> Father...that out of his glorious, unlimited

resources he will give you the mighty inner strengthening of his Holy Spirit. And I pray that Christ will be more and more at home in your hearts, living within you as you trust in him. May your roots go down deep into the soil of God's marvelous love; and may you be able to feel and understand, as all God's children should, how long, how wide, how deep, and how high his love really is; and to experience this love for yourselves, though it is so great that you will never see the end of it or fully know or understand it. And so at last you will be filled up with God himself. (Ephesians 3:14,16-19, TLB)

Wow! Do you still need a reason for joy? Then read Paul's words again…and again until that love begins to root and blossom in your heart.

Earthly word pictures always fall short when trying to describe heavenly truth. Even so, try the following on for size. Imagine that you have inherited some impossibly vast estate—perhaps the size of all of North America. Your estate is filled with soaring mountains, rushing rivers, deep caves, wide prairies, rich pasturelands, deep forests, sparkling lakes, and wide, white beaches where the ocean crashes on purest sand.

It's yours. All yours. You may explore to your heart's content, but you can only experience a fraction of it in your lifetime. You could mount a fast horse and ride and ride for weeks and see only a corner of it.

That is a picture, poor as it may be, of the vastness of His love. *And it is for you.* Love that goes beyond comprehension or knowledge or limited word pictures. What joy to contemplate! And someday soon we will be in eternity, where we will explore that inheritance through the bright, endless morning of heaven and yet never exhaust our journeys. What a wonder!

I love those verses in Ephesians because after Paul makes a faltering attempt to describe the dimensions of this love, he says, "Oh by the way, it's beyond your understanding." It's so great, vast, and incredible, it surpasses the knowledge of people like you and me.

Here's another word picture my friend Joe Wittwer gave me. Trying to grasp the love of God is like attempting to put the Pacific Ocean in a bucket. You could go down to Seaside, Oregon, this afternoon, take your bucket, and dip it into the surf. "What's in the bucket?" I could ask you, and you would reply, "The Pacific Ocean."

You would be right…and terribly wrong.

There might be a little of the Pacific in that bucket, but only an infinitesimal fraction. You could take all the buckets in your city, in your state, in the nation, and have every person dip at the same time, and the ocean wouldn't know it at all. It wouldn't affect the Pacific in the tiniest degree. And by the same token, what you and I have experienced of the Lord's love and joy doesn't come close to exhausting His love!

You say, "But I feel so empty, so dry."

That is why Paul prayed for the Ephesians that they might have the capacity to see and begin to understand. He prayed that their eyes might be opened. And friend, I hope you *will* be filled with God's love and joy, not by the measure of your fullness, but by the measure of His.

Pouring Out His Overabundance of Love

When you begin to see that the cup of your life is much too small to contain the love God keeps pouring into you, you will begin to pour that overabundance of love and great joy into countless thirsty lives all around you. I'm reminded of one more "mailbox story"…but one with a better ending. A young mother wrote:

> One day shortly after my third child was born, I received a note from another young mother, a friend of mine who lived just three blocks from me. We hadn't seen each other all winter.
>
> "Hi, Friend," she wrote, "I think of you often. Someday we'll have time to spend together like in the old days. Keep plugging. I know you're a super mother. See you soon, I hope." It was signed: "your friend on hold, Sue Ann."

The few words lifted my spirits and added a soothing ointment of love to a hectic day. I remember thinking, *Thanks, Sue Ann. I needed that.*

When I went out to mail a note, I noticed a neighbor checking his mailbox. Mr. Williams's head drooped and his pace seemed slower as he shuffled back to his house empty-handed. I hurried back into my own house because I could hear my baby crying, but I couldn't get Mr. Williams off my mind. It wasn't a check he was waiting for; he was quite well-to-do. He was probably looking for some love in his mailbox.

While Meagan drew a picture of a mailbox with a smile in it and Tami drew a rainbow, I wrote a little note. "We are your secret admirers," it began. We added a favorite story and a poem. "Expect to hear from us often," I wrote on the envelope.

The next day my children and I watched Mr. Williams take out his mail and open the envelope right in the driveway. Even at a distance, we could see he was smiling.

My mind began reeling when I thought of all the people who could use smiles in their mailboxes. What about the fifteen-year-old Down's syndrome girl near my parents whose birthday was coming up? The people in the rest home near our house? The invalid woman in our old neighborhood? The endless people I didn't even know who still believe in courtesy and in doing a good job in stores and offices and restaurants? Even on busy days I could find the time to write at least one note.

Notes can be short and should be anonymous. At first, I wanted credit for the notes. But now, writing them in secret adds a sense of adventure. It's more fun. I once overheard talk of "the Phantom Note Lady." They were discussing me, but they didn't know, and I wasn't telling.[1]

One of the best ways I can think of to experience God's joy is to give it away. And the more you give it away, the more you will be filled from heaven's endless reservoirs. Love found a way to bring the world joy...and He has made you part of that plan.

You're in God's Diary

Be joyful, because He is thinking of you. Today. Right now. I heard someone say that if God has a diary, you're in it. If He keeps a yearly calendar, your birthday is circled. If He has a refrigerator, there's a magnet on the door with your picture on it. You're so important to Him, He thinks about you every day. David realized that truth, and his heart overflowed with wonder and joy:

> You saw me before I was born and scheduled each day of my life before I began to breathe. Every day was recorded in your Book!
>
> How precious it is, Lord, to realize that you are thinking about me constantly! I can't even count how many times a day your thoughts turn towards me. And when I waken in the morning, you are still thinking of me! (Psalm 139:16-18, TLB)

Jesus came to earth on that first Christmas so long ago to give us a joy that will remain. Remember what He said to His disciples? "These things I have spoken to you, that My joy may remain in you, and that your joy may be full" (John 15:11, NKJV). We have joy that no one can take away. Even when the mailbox is empty. Even when the choir cancels. Even when the doctor's prognosis isn't good. Even when our fondest dreams are crushed.

Love found a way to bring us joy, a joy that comes not from what we have, but from Who has us.

I heard about a woman not long ago who struggled with a terrible physical handicap resulting from an accident. Her friend, who loved her, struggled with words as she sought to comfort the injured woman. "This tragedy," she said to her friend, "must color all your days."

"Yes," the woman replied, "my days are colored. *But I get to choose the color.*" She had learned how to live in God's promise of joy.

Joy for All the People

Joy! As the angel said, *"Great joy...for all the people."* I love that emphasis on "all people." All people means you. All people means me. All people means your next-door neighbor, the kid with the locker next to yours, the crabby checker at the grocery store, and your Uncle Jim who has never shown any interest in spiritual things. This good news of great joy is for all of us...if only we will receive it.

When you really know the joy, you *feel* the joy. You'll feel like Charles Wesley, who wrote: "O for a thousand tongues to sing, my great Redeemer's praise." You'll say, "I wish I had a thousand tongues—or at least a hundred and fifty. One isn't enough. I wish I was a *choir!*"

So let's sing!

CHAPTER SIX

Love Found a Way... to Counsel Us

For to us a child is born,
to us a son is given,
and the government
will be on his shoulders.
And he will be called
Wonderful Counselor.

ISAIAH 9:6

One of my favorite scenes in the classic Christmas movie *Miracle on 34th Street* is of a little girl brought into a department store to visit Santa Claus. The girl's guardian isn't sure they should have come, for the girl speaks only Dutch. The worried woman doesn't want the girl's tender heart to be disappointed by a Santa who understands only English.

But as Santa takes the little one into his lap, he looks into her eyes and begins gently speaking to her...in Dutch! That little girl's face lights up like a lamp, because Santa knows her language.

That classic scene means a lot to viewers because it's so

69

effective at plucking our heartstrings. But it's fantasy, isn't it? It's just the movies.

Yet I believe that in a far deeper way, we have a heavenly Counselor who speaks to us in our language—at the very point of our need.

Just for Him

Right before Christmas our children's choir—all six hundred little voices—sang for the congregation. There's nothing like listening to kids sing at Christmas. (Don't they say Christmas is for kids?) After they sang that night, I learned that a certain little red-headed boy was in the audience. The youngster was deaf.

As the concert progressed, the lad was at least mildly interested in watching the singing children—but there was no message there for him. How could there be? He couldn't hear any of the words.

Suddenly everything changed. The choir began to sing in this little guy's language, *signing* the words with their hands as well as singing with their voices the beautiful Lanny Wolfe chorus:

> Jesus we crown You with praise,
> Jesus we crown You with praise,
> We love and adore You, bow down before You,
> Jesus we crown You with praise.[1]

The boy suddenly stood up in his seat. His eyes lit up, big as saucers. They were singing to *him!* He could hardly contain his joy. His little hands began to sing as he signed along with the choir.

When the choir finished, that excited little redhead thought the evening had been planned just for him. And I believe in my heart that he was right. God's love doesn't simply speak to crowds; it speaks to individuals. And always it's the Wonderful Counselor who's doing the speaking.

Certified in Every Area

Most of the troubled people I meet in the course of life and ministry aren't looking for a tension-free life, but rather for somewhere to turn for help and advice. Everyone knows that life is filled with challenges and even problems that seem to have no solution. People are crying out for someone to go to, someone to turn to.

Many professional counselors specialize in certain areas of human need. For example, some are trained to deal with depression, others with personality disorders, marriage and family counseling, anger management, or addictions. But God is certified and qualified to counsel in every area. As Isaiah proclaimed, He is a Wonderful Counselor, "the LORD of hosts, who is wonderful in counsel and excellent in guidance" (Isaiah 28:29, NKJV).

What makes Him so effective? That's easy. God knows

everything about everything. He knows just what we need. He knows precisely how we are made.

> As a father has compassion on his children,
>> so the LORD has compassion on those who fear him;
> for he knows how we are formed,
>> he remembers that we are dust. (Psalm 103:13-14)

Although this is gloriously true, I've come to realize that we may never come to understand what a *truly* Wonderful Counselor He is until we're in a difficult, painful, confusing circumstance and seek His counsel with all of our hearts.

I published a book a few years back titled *Meeting God at a Dead End.* That title said a great deal to me, because I believe that the Lord does meet us at those cul-de-sacs of life where there seems to be nowhere to turn, nowhere else to go. And His counsel in those moments is wonderful.

He says to us:

> I will instruct you and teach you
>> in the way which you should go;
> I will counsel you with My eye upon you. (Psalm
>> 32:8, NASB)

In Psalm 73, the psalmist realized what that counsel meant to him and poured out his heart to the Lord:

> You guide me with your counsel,
>> and afterward you will take me into glory.

Whom have I in heaven but you?
> And earth has nothing I desire besides you.
My flesh and my heart may fail,
> but God is the strength of my heart
> and my portion forever. (verses 24-26)

The old commentator Matthew Henry wrote of Jesus, "He is the counselor, for He was intimately acquainted with the counsels of God from eternity, and He gives counsel to the children of men, in which He consults our welfare. He is the wisdom of the Father, and is made of God to us wisdom. He is the wonderful counselor, a wonder or miracle of a counselor; in this, as in other things, He has the preeminence; none teaches like Him."[2] In Christ, love has found a way to reach us and speak to our deepest needs.

He Was There First

During His earthly ministry, Jesus said, "I say only what I hear My Father say; I do only what I see My Father do." When you interpret the Gospels based on that premise, Jesus never went anywhere but that God had already been there, and He never said anything God hadn't already said.

Consider His conversation with the woman at the well, in John 4. At one point He said to her, "Go, call your husband and come back."

"I have no husband," she replied.

Jesus said to her, "You are right when you say you have no husband. The fact is, you have had five husbands, and the man you now have is not your husband. What you have just said is quite true."

"Sir," the woman said, "I can see that you are a prophet." (verses 17-19)

I believe that God had been speaking to this woman for weeks—maybe even months. Perhaps even the night before that conversation, as she lay in her bed, He had been speaking to her conscience, saying, "You don't like this lifestyle. It's as empty as can be. You've been in bed with every man in town. You've fooled around so much you feel like a piece of worthless rag." And in her heart she began thinking, *I don't like this. I don't want to live this way. I don't want to be like this. I wish there were a better way, another way to live.*

And then Jesus showed up. At the well. At high noon.

She had an encounter with Christ and realized that this was the God who had been speaking to her all along. He had already visited with her. She said to Him, "You must be a prophet. How could You know all of those things?" In other words, it wasn't the first time she'd heard them.

I believe that whenever Jesus came to people, God had already been there, communicating with them in the deep places of their hearts.

Counselors with Him

God wants you and me to be the kind of people who not only are counseled by God, but who counsel others according to the direction of the Holy Spirit, believing that God has been dealing with them before we arrived on the scene.

It's an exciting way to live! As you allow Him to use you in this way, you begin to understand how awesome it is to serve and respond to a sovereign God who can direct your words and direct your steps to fulfill His purposes.

Through the years, I can't even count how many people have come up to me after a service and said, "Pastor Ron, there may have been several thousand people here today, but they were just window dressing. I *know* your message today was just for me. God wanted to communicate those words just to me. How did you know those things about me? I feel like you've been reading my mail."

One of my strongest desires as a pastor or counselor is to be one who *confirms* what God is already speaking to people. I believe if we allow ourselves to be filled with the Spirit each day, the Spirit will direct us to say the very words people need to hear.

I really believe that! I've seen it happen more times than I can count. God is working in billions of hearts and lives at the same time all over the world at this very moment. He is continually preparing the ground for the seed of His Word to fall into a life.

That's why I believe there is no such thing as a casual conversation or a chance meeting. I want to be so in tune with the Spirit that I will have the very words that an individual needs to hear at that particular moment in his or her spiritual journey. Maybe it's a word of encouragement. Maybe it's comfort. Maybe it's exhortation. Whatever it is, I want the Counselor to speak through me—and I don't want to miss a single one of His appointments!

In Ephesians 5, Paul cautions us to "be very careful, then, how you live—not as unwise but as wise, making the most of every opportunity, because the days are evil. Therefore do not be foolish, but understand what the Lord's will is" (verses 15-17). To the Colossians he writes: "Let your conversation be always full of grace, seasoned with salt, so that you may know how to answer everyone" (Colossians 4:6). To the Corinthians, he said: "This is what we speak, not in words taught us by human wisdom but in words taught by the Spirit, expressing spiritual truths in spiritual words" (1 Corinthians 2:13).

And yet one more piece of advice may be the most helpful (and convicting) of all:

> Do not let any unwholesome talk come out of
> your mouths, but only what is helpful for build-
> ing others up according to their needs, that it
> may benefit those who listen. (Ephesians 4:29)

God wants to use you and me to do that; He wants to give us the capacity to speak to people and counsel with people, communicating the very things they need to hear.

I heard Billy Graham tell a story on the radio recently about a missionary in India who was on her way to a weekend retreat in the mountains when she saw a beggar sitting by the roadside. Something in her heart whispered that she should stop and tell that man about the love and provision of Jesus Christ. The woman, however, was late for her retreat and hurried on her way.

All through that weekend, she felt convicted about not stopping to speak to that old man. She began praying earnestly that he still might be in the same place when she came down the mountain road on the way home.

As it turned out, he was. That dear woman immediately went over to him and began to tell of him of the love of God in Jesus Christ. As she spoke, tears filled the old man's eyes.

"All my life I have prayed to Him," the man said, "but I didn't know who He was."

The Message Is for You

The Lord knows just what to say to every individual. There was a time when He spoke to each of us about salvation. And through the course of our lives, the Counselor will also speak to us words of conviction, words of correction and adjustment, and words of tenderness and hope. I wonder: Are you giving Him the opportunity to speak to you?

David wrote:

> I will praise the LORD, who counsels me;
> > even at night my heart instructs me.
> I have set the LORD always before me.
> > Because he is at my right hand,
> > I will not be shaken. (Psalm 16:7-8)

Perhaps you have heard people talking about the "love of God" through the years, and somehow it just didn't have any meaning for you. You heard people say, "God loves you" or "Jesus loves you" or "God has a wonderful plan for your life," but it was just so many words.

But then there came a moment when you suddenly realized that message was just for *you*. Suddenly the light came on, and you realized that the whole choir was singing for *you,* that heaven was waiting for *you,* that Jesus Christ died on a Roman cross for *you*. And in that moment your eyes opened wide, your mouth dropped open, and you said, "This is for *me*. This means *me!*"

If that hasn't happened in your life yet, you may count on the fact that God is seeking you even now, at this very moment, through the pages of this book you hold in your hands. Even now you can respond to the Counselor who loves you.

More Than a Counselor

Love found a way to speak to a little red-headed boy, who learned that he, too, could praise the newborn King.

Love found a way to speak to an old beggar along the road in India, giving him a name for the God who had been whispering to his heart through all the years of life.

And love will find a way to speak to you, wherever you are in life, whatever your circumstances, no matter what your need.

How do I know that? Because He's more than a Counselor. He's *Wonderful.*

CHAPTER SEVEN

Love Found a Way... to Change Us

And he will be called...
Mighty God.

ISAIAH 9:6

Did you know that the words "Mighty God" in Isaiah 9:6 really mean "the God-hero"? This striking title of the Lord's might is a constant reminder to us that He will allow nothing at any time to oppose His purpose. He will overcome any and every obstacle as we yield to Him.

Perhaps Mary had this very text in mind when she burst into her joyful song of praise. She realized that what He was doing in her womb would require a mighty act, but then...He had a mighty history! As she made her way toward her cousin's home, she consciously recalled God's power and mighty deeds of days gone by. It was His strength, working in concert with His mercy, that moved her to break into praise as she crossed the threshold of Elizabeth's home:

For the Mighty One has done great things for me—
  holy is his name.
His mercy extends to those who fear him,
  from generation to generation.
He has performed mighty deeds with his arm;
    he has scattered those who are proud in their
      inmost thoughts.
He has brought down rulers from their thrones
    but has lifted up the humble. (Luke 1:49-52)

Mary reminds us that while we can go to friends and relatives and others for help and encouragement, there is only One who can provide both wise counsel *and* the power to change. Jesus is "the Mighty God," and He longs to work His great power in you and me.

That is why Paul told his friends in Philippi: "continue to work out your salvation with fear and trembling, for it is God who works in you to will and to act according to his good purpose" (Philippians 2:12-13). I like the way J. B. Phillips rendered those words in his paraphrase:

> Work out the salvation that God has given you
> with a proper sense of awe and responsibility. For
> it is God who is at work within you, *giving you*
> *the will and the power to achieve his purpose.*
> (emphasis added)

Amazing! Our Lord not only provides the power to change, He provides the *will* to change. Once you make the decision to let Him go to work, He can do *anything* in your life.

Why So Little Change?

Sadly, some of us know precious little about the changes God wants to work in our lives. Why? Because we'd rather rely on ourselves. That's the main reason why the "self-help" industry in our nation continues to explode. We're told that we can take our lives into our own hands, that we are the captain of our own ship, the master of our own destiny. And to a degree, that's true. In fact, we *can* successfully make some personal changes—superficial and external though they may be. We can lose weight, learn a language, improve our skills, bleach our teeth, strengthen our abs, or shorten our nose through plastic surgery.

But what about the inside?

The backwash of "self-help" is that many of us fall into despair, feeling powerless to make significant *internal* changes. Changes in our marriage. Changes in our parenting. Changes in our habits. Changes in our speech. Changes in our attitudes. Changes in our relationships.

It is only God's work within us that can make possible significant change.

A Troubled Teenager

A busy pastor with a wide-reaching television ministry received a phone call from a distraught man he'd never met.

"Pastor?" the man began, "You don't know me, but— well, we watch you on television. I know this is presumptuous, but I'm calling to ask if you'd consider talking to our teenage son. I don't know where else to turn. He's been in quite a bit of trouble and—well, frankly, we can't seem to manage him. We've tried everything, but nothing works. He's watched your program a couple of times, too, Pastor, and knows who you are. Would you consider seeing him?"

It was one of those frustrating times when "no" was on the tip of his tongue and it came out "yes."

Though an effective speaker, this pastor didn't feel confident at all in the counseling room. In fact, someone else on his staff usually handled these kinds of things. But now that he'd agreed to see the lad, he was bound to follow through. In his heart, however, the pastor couldn't help but wonder if the session would only make matters worse. He agreed to an appointment two weeks later, then left on vacation.

While he was away, the congregation voted to redecorate his office as a gift. When he walked in the door upon his return, his eyes lit up to see fresh paint, new carpet, and some lovely new furniture.

As it happened, the very first visitor in his newly refurbished office was the troubled teenager. You could read "attitude" in this young man from a block away. Everything about his dress, his posture, and his personal appearance shouted "rebel"! The boy slouched into one of the brand-new chairs, his face as impassive as stone.

Oh, man, the pastor thought to himself. *How did I get into this one? Why am I doing this?*

He tried to warm the boy up with a little conversation.

"So...um, what do you think of the Lakers this year?"

"I hate the Lakers."

"Z'at right? Well then, do you have a favorite basketball team?"

"I hate basketball."

Every question the pastor asked got a quick "yeah" or "no" answer.

That was bad enough. What was much, much worse was the young man's appalling habit of hacking and *spitting* on the brand-new carpet. Anger surged up within this minister and he thought, *I can't believe this! I'm gonna throw this kid out on his ear.*

Then in a flash it hit him. This young man wasn't spitting on the carpet...he was spitting on his parents.

Without even thinking it through, the pastor got up from his chair, walked over by the boy's chair, knelt down and put a hand on the boy's arm. "Son," he said, "you may not believe this, and that's okay. You don't have to believe a single thing I say. But I want you to know I love you. I really care about you. What's more, I *believe* in you."

The obnoxious young man with the face of chiseled stone looked at the kneeling pastor and his eyes suddenly filled with tears. With a voice he could no longer control, he said, "Man, I have everything you could ever want. But in all my life I've never heard anyone say, 'I love you. I believe in you.'"

Before that session was through, the young man knelt down with the pastor and asked Jesus into his heart. He was never the same again. Love found a way to change him forever.

Opportunities for Faith

Isaiah 64:4 speaks of a God "who acts on behalf of those who wait for him." When Paul quotes the prophet in 1 Corinthians, he changes the verse to read: "for those who *love* him." In the apostle's mind, waiting appears to be the same as love; if you don't wait, you prove you don't love. On the other hand, if you're willing to wait, you demonstrate your love, because love waits.

Ephesians 2:10 tell us that "we are God's workmanship, created in Christ Jesus to do good works, which God prepared in advance for us to do." The word for workmanship is the Greek word *poiema*. We get our word "poem" and "poetry" from the same root. It is a term signifying something manufactured—a product or a design produced by an artisan. *Poiema* emphasizes God as the Master Designer—both of creation and of the redeemed believer, His new creation. Working within us, He brings balance and symmetry, order and discipline. We are God's poem, His work of art.

And that's true even though life may be filled with difficult situations and challenging tasks. The Lord doesn't tell us in advance what these will be; they simply come upon us, and in each instance we must choose whether to rely on His power or seek to go it alone in our own strength.

As we've already seen, when the Lord sent His disciples across the lake ahead of Him, He knew very well a storm was on its way. He knew they would strain at the oars. He knew they would be in danger. But He also knew He had the power to walk right into the storm and meet them in their need. Would they call on Him? Would they lean on Him? Would they trust in Him?

Shortly before that incident took place, our Lord gave Philip a chance to lean on His power in a different setting. (How I love this story!)

> Jesus crossed to the far shore of the Sea of Galilee…and a great crowd of people followed him because they saw the miraculous signs he had performed on the sick. Then Jesus went up on a mountainside and sat down with his disciples. The Jewish Passover Feast was near.
>
> When Jesus looked up and saw a great crowd coming toward him, he said to Philip, "Where

shall we buy bread for these people to eat?" He
asked this only to test him, for he already had in
mind what he was going to do. (John 6:1-6)

What a curve ball to throw at old Philip! The Lord
already knew He was going to provide and how He would
accomplish it…but He gave this man an opportunity to step
out into the scary realms of walking by faith. Would Philip
believe Jesus Christ had the power to move into this situation
and change it?

No, not quite yet. Like most of us, he had some more
growing to do:

Philip answered him, "Eight months' wages
would not buy enough bread for each one to
have a bite!"…
Jesus said, "Have the people sit down."
(verses 7,10)

Situations roll across our daily lives like wind-driven
clouds. It may be a storm that threatens to swamp your boat.
It may be feeding five thousand hungry people with a sack
lunch. It may be staring up at the towering walls of Jericho.
It may be facing an unyielding habit or temptation that has
plagued you for years and which you are powerless to change.
He doesn't tell us what we will face. He simply gives us
opportunity after opportunity to lean on Him. No matter

what our circumstances, He will make a way for us. He will give us the will and the power to change, to achieve His purpose. We need faith because—finite beings that we are—we just can't know what's ahead of us...whether good or bad.

Living in Chapter Six

A friend of mine told me he often counsels troubled people to turn to 2 Kings chapter 6. Curious, I looked up the chapter. Scanning through those verses, I thought, *You've got to be kidding! Why would you want someone who was troubled or struggling to read such an account? What's encouraging about THAT?*

Then he explained it to me. In the narrative of that chapter, the nation of Israel is besieged by foes and the people within the city of Samaria are literally starving—even mothers resort to cannibalism.

The king of Israel, a rebel against the Lord as all his predecessors had been, scoffed at the thought of seeking help from God. In utter unbelief he said, "This disaster is from the LORD. Why should I wait for the LORD any longer?" (2 Kings 6:33).

Many people who have sat in my office have asked that very question. "This situation in my life has been going on and on. Nothing seems to change. Why should I wait on the Lord? Why should I trust in Him?"

At the beginning of 2 Kings 7, however, Elisha sends this message to the king by the hand of an Israelite officer. "About this time tomorrow, you will be able to buy seven quarts of flour for less than half of an ounce of silver. You will also be able to buy 13 quarts of barley for the same price. That's all you will have to pay for those things at the gate of Samaria" (7:1, NIrV).

The officer refused to believe Elisha. He couldn't conceive of such a thing happening. How could God deal with a powerful, intractable enemy and bring such cheap, abundant food to the city *overnight?* He replied to Elisha, "Look, even if the LORD should open the floodgates of the heavens, could this happen?"

" 'You will see it with your own eyes,' answered Elisha, 'but you will not eat any of it!' " (2 Kings 7:2).

If only the king's bitter, cynical officer could have read chapter 7, he would not have scoffed at God's ability to radically change the situation of his dying city. And if only the king could have read 2 Kings 7, he, too, would have known why it was worth waiting for the Lord; he would have seen a mighty, miraculous provision. He would have known that God would indeed open the floodgates of heaven! But the king and his messenger were stuck in chapter 6 and did not believe.

That's true of all of us, isn't it? We get into a "chapter 6" kind of jam and can't begin to imagine how the Lord could work in such a situation. We become discouraged over our weaknesses and failures and can't conceive how the Lord could change us and do a work of grace and power in our hearts.

We get stuck in chapter 6.

But we never know what's in chapter 7, do we?

We never know what God is planning.

We have no idea what God's "surprise ending" might be.

Like Philip, we can't see around the situation. We get out our calculator and count heads and say, "We're in major trouble here. We could never feed such a mob of people. We don't begin to have enough money or enough resources."

But like Philip, we forget just Who it is who stands beside us:

His name shall be called…Mighty God.

What's the Use?

Maybe this is a "chapter 6" Christmas for you. The ghosts of Christmas Past have left you cynical about Christmas Present—and you hold out little hope for Christmas Future. You can't seem to shake that dark cloud that's been following you. It seems like the Christmas lights dim whenever you walk into the room. You've found yourself thinking, *What's the use? Why should I wait for Him any longer? Why should I hold out hope for change in my life?*

Just remember, He knows you're in chapter 6. He is the mighty God, the God Hero, and chapter 7 is near at hand. *Believe Him. Wait for Him.* He can turn the pages in your life and bring you to a conclusion beyond your comprehension.

He knows just what He is going to do. My friend, count on it: Love *will* find a way.

CHAPTER EIGHT

Love Found a Way... to Adopt Us

And he will be called...
Everlasting Father.

ISAIAH 9:6

"For unto us a child is born," said the prophet, "unto us a son is given...and His name shall be called...*everlasting Father.*"

Through that first Christmas, God found a way to adopt us. He's a Father who loves surprises and who loves to give gifts. Many of those gifts arrive on our doorstep here in this life, and many more wait for that day when we walk into His embrace. But of all the things that delight us on earth and await us in heaven, nothing compares to the fact that He made us His children through the gift of His own Son.

Chosen and Loving It

My dear friend Joe Wittwer is not only a much-loved pastor in Spokane, Washington, he and his wife, Laina, are model parents. Whenever I'm around them, I'm both convicted and encouraged by the love and commitment they show to one another—and especially to their children.

There are five children in the Wittwer family. The two oldest boys were adopted, arriving in Joe and Laina's arms when were two and three days old, respectively. Joe's a pleasant, easygoing man who isn't easy to rile. But don't ever make the mistake of saying that Joe has two adopted children and three of his own.

He will quickly set you straight. "*All* of 'em are mine," he will tell you. "They belong to us. We just got them in different ways."

Christmas is a riotous occasion in the Wittwer household. Joe says, "I love giving gifts to my kids. But of all the gifts I could have ever given to my two oldest boys, none will match the first one: *I made them my sons.* That's the greatest gift of love I could ever give them."

And believe me, those boys know it.

I'm reminded of the little guy who came home from school crying. When his mother asked what was wrong, he told her he didn't feel special. He was sad because he'd been born into his family, rather than adopted, like one of his school chums. It seems that his friend had parents who knew how to make their adopted son feel very, very secure. He had proudly explained, "My mom and dad told me I am special. You know why? Because they *chose* me. Other kids aren't chosen. Their parents just have to take whatever they get!"

The Greatest Gift of All

After all the things God has done for me, after all the miracles, all the open doors, all the healing, all the deliverances, all the provision, all the constant, never-ceasing care—nothing compares to the fact that He made me His child. He has given me wonderful gifts through the years and showered me with more blessings than I can number. But nothing moves me more than knowing *He chose me.* He made me part of His own family. That's the greatest gift of all.

However you want to look at that amazing phrase, "He chose me," it continues to surprise.

HE *(God! The mighty Creator of nameless, numberless galaxies, the sovereign Ruler of the universe, the great King above all kings, the Father of our Lord Jesus Christ, and the inventor of Christmas)* chose me.

He CHOSE me *(picked me out, selected me, preferred me, wanted me, made plans for me before I drew my first breath).*

He chose ME *(a rebel, a sinner, a man with no heart or time for God, a man with no prospects, no hope, and nothing to recommend him).*

Jesus said, "You did not choose me, but I chose you and appointed you to go and bear fruit" (John 15:16). Paul wrote: "Consider what he has done—before the foundation of the world he chose us to become, in Christ, his holy and blameless children living within his constant care. He planned, in his purpose of love, that we should be adopted as his own children through Jesus Christ—that we might learn to praise that glorious generosity of his which has made us welcome in the everlasting love he bears toward the Beloved" (Ephesians 1:4-7, Phillips).

My friend Joe says about his family, "They're all my kids—they just came to us in different ways." That's true with all of us in the body of Christ, isn't it? Some come to Him as little children, like Timothy. Paul said of him, "But as for you, continue in what you have learned and have become convinced of…and how from infancy you have known the holy Scriptures, which are able to make you wise for salvation through faith in Christ Jesus" (2 Timothy 3:14-15). Others, like the man crucified alongside the Lord Jesus, come to Christ at the last possible moment, gasping, "Jesus, remember me," as they slip from this life.

Some turn to Jesus naturally, as children running fast as their legs will carry them into His open arms; others turn to Him only after great heartache and crisis, when the storms of life have stripped everything else away. Some come from a culture and home life surrounded by the Bible and the things of God; others come from extremely hostile cultures and backgrounds where Christianity is like a strange, alien thing. Some come to Christ as preschoolers. Others as teens. Others as adults rescued out of a destructive, shameful lifestyle.

Some come into the kingdom from environments where they have been loved and affirmed and respected. Others come to Jesus as wounded, abused, emotionally broken individuals who through all their years have never known a loving word or a tender touch. Some have lived lives of gross sin, and others have lived in a way that would almost make you think they didn't need Him. As in our Lord's parable, some will enter heaven having worked for the kingdom through hardship and trials and the heat of the day, while others will "hire on" at the last minute, just before quitting time. Paul said it like this:

> Brothers, think of what you were when you were called. Not many of you were wise by human standards; not many were influential; not many were of noble birth. But God chose the foolish things of the world to shame the wise; God chose the weak things of the world to shame the strong. He chose the lowly things of this world and the despised things—and the things that are not—to nullify the things that are. (1 Corinthians 1:26-28)

We come through the One Door in different ways at different times and from different backgrounds. He calls us from various places and speaks to us in various ways—to some with a whisper, some with a shout, some with a warning, and some with a song. But once we step through that cross-shaped door, we're just His kids. He makes no distinctions between us—son or daughter, young or old, rich or poor, broken or whole.

David wrote:

> For if my father and mother should abandon me,
> you would welcome and comfort me. (Psalm
> 27:10, TLB)

When Our Hearts Fail

Because of the circumstances out of which we were adopted, many of us feel insecure from time to time. We relive some old memories. We feel some old hurts. We're troubled by old fears from days long ago. We remember the dark seasons of our rebellion and our destructive behavior. We recall how hateful we were toward God and hurtful toward others.

David cringed to recall some of those things and prayed, "Remember not the sins of my youth and my rebellious ways; according to your love remember me, for you are good, O LORD" (Psalm 25:7). At another time, he admitted: "For troubles without number surround me; my sins have overtaken me, and I cannot see. They are more than the hairs of my head, and my heart fails within me" (Psalm 40:12).

Why does our heart fail within us? Because we feel unworthy of His love, unsuited for salvation, and undeserving of all the kindnesses He lavishes upon us. We're like the prodigal son who stumbles, dirty and ashamed, into his father's arms and blurts out, "Father, I have sinned against heaven and against you. I am no longer worthy to be called your son" (Luke 15:21).

The enemy actively encourages such thoughts. He whispers, "You call yourself a child of *God?* And this is how you act? You've failed once too often—He doesn't want you anymore. Why, you may not belong to God at all."

To counter the lies of the adversary, God has sent us "the Spirit of adoption." One of the major ministries of the Holy Spirit within us is to continually convince us and remind us that we are chosen by God, adopted members of His very own family.

Paul wrote:

> So you should not be like cowering, fearful slaves.
> You should behave instead like God's very own
> children, adopted into his family—calling him
> "Father, dear Father." For his Holy Spirit speaks
> to us deep in our hearts and tells us that we are
> God's children. And since we are his children, we
> will share his treasures—for everything God gives
> to his Son, Christ, is ours, too. (Romans 8:15-17,
> NLT)

That's the ministry of God's Holy Spirit. That's His never-ending task. That's the joy of His life. He speaks continually, saying, "You're special to God. He handpicked you. He chose you out of the whole world. You are wanted. You are loved."

> Because you are sons, God sent the Spirit of his
> Son into our hearts, the Spirit who calls out,
> "*Abba,* Father." So you are no longer a slave, but
> a son; and since you are a son, God has made
> you also an heir. (Galatians 4:6-7)

That's the Spirit's job! It's not our job to remind ourselves that God loves us; it's *His* job. In a thousand ways He is continually telling us how much He loves us and how dear we are to Him.

No wonder Isaiah tells us God is an *everlasting* Father! As a pastor, I hear sad stories of parents estranged from their own children. I hear of fathers or mothers who become angry and cut off communication with sons and daughters or change their wills to leave children out of the inheritance.

Maybe you've seen the bumper stickers on some of those big RVs rolling down the highway: "We're spending our children's inheritance." That's not true of our Father! He is saving our inheritance for that best of all days when we will step into the brightness of His presence. Peter reminds us:

> God has reserved for his children the priceless gift
> of eternal life; it is kept in heaven for you, pure

and undefiled, beyond the reach of change and decay. And God, in his mighty power, will make sure that you get there safely to receive it, because you are trusting him. It will be yours in that coming last day for all to see. So be truly glad! There is wonderful joy ahead, even though the going is rough for a while down here. (1 Peter 1:4-6, TLB)

God says to us, "I have made you My child and My heir. I will not abandon you. I will not give up on you. I will not find anyone I love better and walk away." He wants a relationship with you that never ends.

Divorce Isn't in the Picture

Unfortunately, our perspective on love isn't everlasting, but often short term and temporary. Parents divorce one another. Kids divorce their parents. Maybe you know what it was like to grow up without a mom or without a dad.

My own father left the family shortly after I was born. I had a wonderful mom and a stepfather who came into the picture to provide for us, but I never experienced that bond with a dad who loved me. I never knew what it was to have a dad play ball with me or take me fishing or come to my basketball games.

My father left long before I ever got to know him. When

I needed him, he was absent. When I longed for him, he was out of reach. When I wanted to lean on him, there was nothing there. When as a lonely boy I cried out for him in my heart, nobody answered.

Life in today's world tells us again and again that love is temporary. Love is passing. It is fickle and selfish and spun of gossamer. Just tune into a country-western station for a few minutes and listen to the trail of broken hearts, broken vows, and broken dreams. God described our human love like this: "Your love is like the morning mist, like the early dew that disappears" (Hosea 6:4).

But the everlasting Father will never leave us. We will enjoy and thrill under His care and tenderness and companionship forever and ever.

He's My Big Brother!

We would do well to pause long enough this Christmas to ponder the amazing fact that although God is the patriarch of a family as numberless as the sands of the seashore, as uncountable as the stars of the sky—in fact, a brood so enormous that He Himself calls it "a great multitude that no one could count, from every nation, tribe, people, and language" (Revelation 7:9)—He has but one "birth Son," our Lord Jesus Christ. The translators of the *King James Bible* called Him "the only begotten Son of God," while more recently the *New International Version* opted for the title, "the One and Only" (John 1:14).

And yet God has promised to treat every one of His adopted kids just like He treats His "One and Only." That is why we can rightly be called "co-heirs with Christ" (Romans 8:17). That is why the Lord can promise through the apostle John that we will "reign" with Christ, even sitting on His throne with Him (Revelation 20:6; 3:21). That is why we can be called the "brothers" of Jesus (Hebrews 2:11-12). In fact, God has so closely identified us with His "One and Only" that His Word says we have been "clothed" with Christ (Galatians 3:27).

That is the sort of "everlasting Father" we have! When you were alone and in need, He determined to become your Parent and Provider. And what happened in Bethlehem so long ago made it all possible.

> How great is the love the Father has lavished on us, that we should be called children of God! And that is what we are! The reason the world does not know us is that it did not know him. Dear friends, now we are children of God, and what we will be has not yet been made known. But we know that when he appears, we shall be like him, for we shall see him as he is. (1 John 3:1-2)

CHAPTER NINE

Love Found a Way...
to Bring Us Peace

And he will be called...
Prince of Peace.

ISAIAH 9:6

So often our first response to anxiety is to run to some expert. A doctor. A counselor. A financial analyst. A psychologist. A mediation service. Those people certainly perform good services and have valid information to share. But I'll tell you this: They won't take the load off your shoulders. They won't bring you peace. Frankly, peace is something money can't buy.

It's a gift.

In fact, it's a Christmas gift.

It began with a little baby breaking through the curtain of darkness and despair and becoming a great light in our cynical, troubled world. The prophet said His name would be called "Prince of Peace."

Are Answers the Answer?

Sometimes you will hear people say, "If I could just have the answers to my questions…if I just knew the real story…if I just had the facts—even if the news is bad news—I would finally have some peace."

I'm not so sure.

I understand what they're saying—to a point. We have concerns about our loved ones, our health, our career, our finances, and our relationships. Our minds seem wired to work and work on a topic, worrying it as a dog worries an old slipper. We can't put the thing down until it's chewed to tatters. We exhaust ourselves trying to see through walls, peer into the future, dissect people's words, discern hidden motives, or uncover some perplexing event from the past.

David described that state of mind well in one of his psalms. He wrote: "How long must I wrestle with my thoughts and every day have sorrow in my heart? How long will my enemy triumph over me?" (Psalm 13:2).

Personally, I don't believe that peace comes with "having the answers." I don't believe we receive comfort by knowing the full story or gaining the facts or acquiring knowledge. It's usually been true in my experience that for every answer I gain, twelve new questions spring up. If you find the reason "why this happened," it will only set you on fire to know "then why in the world did *that* happen?"

It's a humbling thing, but human understanding cannot put life in a logical order. Finite minds such as ours cannot piece together the jigsaw puzzle. How could we? We've never seen the big picture on the box! We pick up a puzzle piece here and there and don't have any idea if it's a piece of lake or a piece of sky. We could spend the rest of our years digging through the pieces, trying to match them up and discern some kind of pattern. Like David, we wrestle with our thoughts every day and go to bed with sorrow.

In my life, I have found that peace doesn't come from obtaining the answers, but from giving the situation to Jesus Christ, the Prince of Peace. I'm not talking about some kind of grim fatalism here, where you say, "Oh well, what will be will be." No, there is a vast difference between surrendering to the circumstances and surrendering to God. When you give the situation to God, peace results because *He becomes responsible for the outcome.* If you don't give it to God, in essence you're making yourself responsible for the outcome.

For the last eighteen years, I've dealt with a disease called chronic lymphocytic leukemia. I've had it since I was thirty-six; I am now fifty-four. The doctors say I've outlived my life expectancy by many years.

Questions? Of course I've had questions. Who wouldn't? I've wondered why He has allowed it. I've pondered why there hasn't been healing. I've asked myself how He might want to use this illness or what He might want me to learn.

Frankly, I haven't had all the answers I've desired—nor do I have them even now. But I will tell you this: I've had something better than "the answers."

I've had the Prince of Peace.

He has been my Companion through it all. My friend, it is far, far better to have the companionship of Jesus Christ than the answers to your questions—*whatever those questions may be.*

His presence and His peace are more desirable than "answers." There is nothing better in all of life than His companionship. The nearness of God makes anything in life endurable.

The old preacher Charles Spurgeon once said, "If you do not come to Him, you will receive no peace; if you do not keep near Him, you will retain no peace; and if you do not grow nearer and nearer to Him, you will miss much of the peace that you might have. Abide in Christ Jesus, and let Him abide in you, and you shall have abundance of peace."

It's No Secret

Many before me have made this same discovery. It's not a secret as much as it is a key. The key is available to all who would pick it up and use it, and it isn't hidden in some dark corner somewhere; bright neon signs and billboards the size of New Jersey direct our attention to it. So why don't more of us seek the Prince of Peace rather than "answers"? I suppose it's related to what G. K. Chesterton once said: "The trouble is not that Christianity has been tried and been found wanting; the trouble is that it has been found difficult and left untried."

Yes, it can be difficult to let go of our questions so that we can lean on the Prince of Peace. But many are those who can testify to the wisdom of doing so!

Mary, the mother of Jesus, didn't have all the answers. But she did have peace.

To the angel's wondrous, troubling message, Mary said, "I am the Lord's servant.... May it be to me as you have said" (Luke 1:38).

It didn't make a particle of earthly sense. Talk about a puzzle! A pregnancy with no sexual relations? A virgin conception? And what would people say? Of course they would assume she had been unfaithful, immoral. For the rest of her life, she would probably carry that shadow. What would Joseph say? Wouldn't he be crushed when she gave him the news? Wouldn't he assume the worst? There had to be a lot of confusion. There had to be fear in the pit of her stomach. What would happen to her marriage plans? Was life over— or was it just beginning? *How could this be?*

Yet after a moment's consideration, she gave it over to the only One with answers. In trust, she said to the angel, "I'm the Lord's handmaiden. If that's what He has in mind for me, then I don't have to understand. Just let it be so."

I can't help but notice that she asked only one question: "How can this be?" After that, as far as Scripture reveals, she never questioned anything again. The great counsels of God were beyond her; she simply submitted to His will...and found peace.

Abraham, the man called "the friend of God," didn't have all the answers. But he did have peace.

Out of the blue, the Lord he had loved and followed through life had asked him to offer his own dear son—the boy whose name meant "laughter"—as a burnt offering at a designated place. Scripture says, "On the third day Abraham looked up and saw the place in the distance. He said to his servants, 'Stay here with the donkey while I and the boy go over there. We will worship and then we will come back to you'" (Genesis 22:4-5).

This brokenhearted father couldn't conceive why God would ask such a thing. This didn't seem like the God he knew at all. But he didn't demand an answer from the Lord. He didn't try to figure it out. He simply obeyed, reasoning that somehow God would put it all together—even if He had to raise Isaac from the dead.

Mary and Abraham knew something I've had to learn through the years: When you walk with God and obey His voice, God becomes responsible for your life. The peace comes when you've given your hurts and perplexities over into His hands.

Habakkuk didn't have all the answers. But he did have peace.

In the book that bears his name, the prophet asked the Lord some deep and searching questions. He received answers—but they were almost more than he could bear. The glimpse into the future he'd been given left him shocked and devastated. In the end, he simply bowed to a wisdom so much greater than his own:

> Though the fig tree does not bud
>> and there are no grapes on the vines,
> though the olive crop fails
>> and the fields produce no food,
> though there are no sheep in the pen
>> and no cattle in the stalls,
> yet I will rejoice in the LORD,
>> I will be joyful in God my Savior.
>> (Habakkuk 3:17-18)

At last the prophet knelt at the Lord's feet in worship, saying, in effect, "Lord, I don't know what's going to happen. I don't know what will become of me, my family, or my nation. But I do know You! And You are my joy and delight—You are my peace—no matter what happens in my life."

The apostle Paul didn't have all the answers. But he did have peace.

Acts 23 describes how Paul had just been snatched by Roman soldiers out of the clutches of a murderous mob. Scripture says the "dispute became so violent that the commander was afraid Paul would be torn to pieces by them" (verse 10). In custody in the Roman barracks, Paul had every reason to wonder what would happen to him. He probably had lots of questions. But listen to what happened:

> The following night the Lord stood near Paul and said, "Take courage! As you have testified about me in Jerusalem, so you must also testify in Rome." (verse 11)

Paul found peace in the Prince of Peace even when the walls closed in on him, even when the answers didn't come. He didn't get out of jail the night he was attacked by the mob. In fact, he ended up being incarcerated for over two years. Think of the plans put on hold! Think of the dreams shelved! Think of the loneliness and frustration! Yet Jesus Himself had told him, "Take courage. I have a plan for your life, Paul, and you're right on course."

Years later, near the end of his life, in a deeper, darker prison than he'd ever endured, suffering from the cold, from desertion by his friends, and from uncountable aches and pains due to his beatings, the apostle wrote: "That is why I am suffering as I am. Yet I am not ashamed, because *I know whom I have believed*, and am convinced that he is able to guard what I have entrusted to him for that day" (2 Timothy 1:12, emphasis added).

Paul knew he would never leave that dungeon alive. But he placed his confidence in Jesus Christ, saying, "I know whom I have believed." And that was all he *needed* to know.

What was the key to Paul's confidence in those frightening situations? He revealed it to the Philippians—and to you and me: "Do not be anxious about anything, but in everything, by prayer and petition, with thanksgiving, present your requests to God. And the peace of God, which transcends all understanding, will guard your hearts and your minds in Christ Jesus" (Philippians 4:6-7).

Not once does Paul promise you'll receive answers for all your questions. The peace he describes doesn't come from obtaining information—or even from a change of circumstances! The change is one of *focus*.

Paul is saying, "I don't have peace because I have all the answers or received what I wanted, but rather because I've given it all to Him. And the moment I gave it to Him, I began to feel a sense of peace and rest, because I know He's going to care for it all."

Peter didn't have all the answers. But he had peace.

To a group of Christians undergoing fierce persecution and suffering, the apostle set forth both an invitation and a warning.

First, the invitation: "Cast all your anxiety on him because he cares for you" (1 Peter 5:7). That's a quotable verse, isn't it? You've seen it written in calligraphy and framed in people's homes or offices. You've heard it sung in songs and praise choruses.

Sometimes, however, that thought gets separated from the verses that immediately follow. And they were meant to go together!

> Be self-controlled and alert. Your enemy the devil prowls around like a roaring lion looking for someone to devour. Resist him, standing firm in the faith, because you know that your brothers throughout the world are undergoing the same kind of sufferings. (verses 8-9)

When this passage tells us that the devil, prowling like a roaring lion, is looking for someone to devour, it's in the context of "cast all your anxiety on Him."

Do you know what that says to me? The devil feeds on our worry! It attracts "the roaring lion" like raw meat. And as he prowls around, he smells it—and hurries to its source. Satan wants to keep you in a state of agitation. He wants to see your life filled with anxieties, cares, worries, and concerns. He doesn't want you to experience peace, and he certainly wants to separate you from the Prince of Peace.

The fact is, *anything that you haven't surrendered to God becomes lion bait.* It might be your marriage. It might be your career. It might be your bills or your mother-in-law or a feud with your neighbor or a thousand other things. If you haven't surrendered it to God, if you haven't cast all your cares and anxieties on him every morning as you get up and every evening as you climb into bed, you've left out bait for the lion. You'll become aware of great conflict and struggle in that very area. That's where your greatest lack of peace will be.

Peter knew all about lion bait, and he knew the best way to avoid setting it out was to give his cares and anxieties to the Prince of Peace—also known as the Lion of the tribe of Judah. Since *that* Lion will chase away that other lion every single time, we are left with the one thing we most need: Peace!

Worth Lingering Over

The prophet Isaiah was so taken by his vision of the Prince of Peace that he did something at the end of this famous Christmas passage that he didn't do with any of the other titles he used to describe the coming Messiah. He lingered over it, expanded on it, reveled in it. So he wrote:

> Of the increase of his government and peace
>> there will be no end....
> The zeal of the LORD Almighty
>> will accomplish this. (Isaiah 9:7)

When the Lord Almighty is zealous that the peace of the Prince of Peace increase and multiply, you can bet your last dollar that peace will most certainly rule! As the prophet said in another place, "All your sons will be taught by the LORD, and great will be your children's peace" (Isaiah 54:13).

Isaiah proclaims to us that the day is coming when the whole world will bow before Jesus and call Him by His royal title, the Prince of Peace.

But you know what? You and I get to do it right now! And all because Love found a way.

CHAPTER TEN

Love Found a Way...
to Bring Us Hope

Isaiah says,
"The Root of Jesse will spring up,
one who will arise to rule over the nations;
the Gentiles will hope in him."

ROMANS 15:12

Hope is a Christmas word. The season rings with hope, from the hopes of a seven-year-old boy ("I hope I get my bike!") to the hopes of an expectant mother ("I hope the baby comes before Christmas!") to the hopes of a seasoned department-store Santa ("I hope this kid's bottom is wet because of the snow!").

But is this the kind of hope our Lord meant to give us when Jesus came to our planet as a tiny baby so long ago? Hardly. In our language, "hope" has become little more than a wishy-washy verb.

It has a kind of thin, sugar-frosted coating around it that may make us think of making a birthday wish before blowing out the candles, or Jiminy Cricket singing, "When you wish upon a star…" It's nice but weak. Pleasant but nothing to hold on to. Sweet but insubstantial. Cheerful but it could never pull you out of deep trouble or hurt.

We will say, "I hope you have a nice vacation," or "I hope to lose a little weight," or "I hope it all turns out for the best." But we have no confidence that any of those things will really happen. It was just something agreeable to say at the moment.

This weak, pale English word bears little resemblance to the mighty noun that rises like a towering mountain out of the pages of the New Testament.

When we talk about the kind of hope Jesus brings to us because of Christmas, we're not talking about some light-weight, frail, and flimsy emotional feeling that gets tossed with the discarded wrapping paper.

No, the Bible's brand of hope is very different. This is a hope shot through with confidence. This is hope so muscu-lar it can pull you out of a deep pit. This is hope so powerful it can anchor your life—keeping you secure in the highest waves and strongest storms. This is hope stronger than death—a hope upon which you'd stake your life…and your eternity.

Like a Steel Cable

In the New Testament, hope is that which you anticipate with assurance and pleasure. It is a strong and stable expectation—like a thick steel cable—linking you to the promises and character of God Himself. It pertains to the unseen and the future and describes a happy anticipation of good.

Speaking of our hope in Christ, the writer to the Hebrews tells us: "This hope we have as an anchor of the soul, a hope both sure and steadfast and one which enters within the veil, where Jesus has entered as a forerunner for us, having become a high priest forever" (Hebrews 6:19-20, NASB).

Why is the word so strong? Why is it "sure and steadfast"? Why is it an anchor for our soul? Because of the *object* upon which that hope is fixed. This isn't hope for hope's sake; this is hope centered in an almighty, loving Lord. Paul called himself "an apostle of Christ Jesus by the command of God our Savior and of Christ Jesus our hope" (1 Timothy 1:1). In Romans 15:13, he speaks of God as "the God of hope." In other words, He is the Author of hope—the genuine article that makes every other use of "hope" seem thin as a winter shadow.

Peter tells us that God "has given us new birth into a living hope through the resurrection of Jesus Christ from the dead, and into an inheritance that can never perish, spoil or fade" (1 Peter 1:3-4). You might be on your deathbed, but in that very moment you can grip a hope so strong and alive that its reality will sweep you right into the presence of the living God.

Hope is that which connects us to God and to heaven,

His dwelling place. Look at this paraphrase of the verses we just read:

> So that…we who are refugees from this dying
> world might have a source of strength, and might
> grasp the hope that he holds out to us. This hope
> we hold as the utterly reliable anchor for our
> souls, fixed in the innermost shrine of Heaven,
> where Jesus has already entered on our behalf.
> (Hebrews 6:18-20, Phillips)

Not long ago I read this amazing story:

> Years ago a submarine was rammed by a ship off
> the coast of Massachusetts. It sank immediately.
> The entire crew was trapped in a prison house
> of death. Every effort was made to rescue the
> crew, but all ultimately failed. Near the end of
> the ordeal, a deep-sea diver, who was doing
> everything in his power to find a way for the
> crew's release, thought he heard a tapping on
> the steel wall of the sunken sub. He placed his
> helmet up against the side of the vessel and he
> realized it was Morse Code. He attached him-
> self to the side and he spelled out in his mind
> the message being tapped from within. It was

repeating the same question. The question
was, from within: "Is…there…any…
hope?"

With great sadness he signaled back:
"Hope…in…God…alone."[1]

Apart from Jesus Christ coming to this world as our
Savior, apart from His birth that night outside the little village of Bethlehem, our situation would be just like that of
those doomed sailors sitting in the darkness on the bottom of
the sea. We would have nothing to look forward to but certain death and separation from God. We would have no
more hope of obtaining heaven than those poor servicemen
had of swimming to the surface. Scripture says that you and
I were "separate from Christ…*without hope* and without God
in the world" (Ephesians 2:12, emphasis added).

But now?

But now in Christ Jesus you who once were far
away have been brought near through the blood
of Christ.

For he himself is our peace. (verses 13-14)

Hope tells us that no matter what our situation, we can
rest in the hands of a sovereign God who loves us very much.
With David, we can speak to our own soul and say:

Find rest, O my soul, in God alone;
  my hope comes from him.
He alone is my rock and my salvation;
  he is my fortress, I will not be shaken.
      (Psalm 62:5-6)

Why Put Our Hope in Him?

Jesus came not only to bring us hope, but also to demonstrate why we should put our hope in Him. Let's focus briefly on four of those reasons for putting our hope and trust in Him.

1. Because He has a long-term plan for my life

Jesus is up to something. He is involved in my life for the long haul. As Paul told us, "I am sure that God who began the good work within you will keep right on helping you grow in his grace until his task within you is finally finished on that day when Jesus Christ returns" (Philippians 1:6, TLB).

He is taking us someplace. He is working to bring about change within us. And who is better qualified than He? He has the desire to do it. He has the power and sovereignty and wisdom to do it. He knows us intimately and loves us dearly.

He is not the God of "quick fixes." Scripture says that He is Alpha and Omega, the Beginning and the End, the Author and the Finisher of our faith. He does not walk away from His investments—and He already invested heavily in your life when He sent His Son to die for you. He has long-term plans for you, in both time and in the eternal morning on the other side. He's not going to give up. As He told Israel, "For I know the plans I have for you…plans to prosper you and not to harm you, plans to give you hope and a future" (Jeremiah 29:11).

If He loved you and chose you and redeemed you, *He has a plan for you.* You can depend upon it. You can fix your hope upon it. God never gives up on us because He knows there's a better day ahead. He can see it at this very moment. He *knows.* This is where I am today, but He already knows what His grace and kindness will one day accomplish in my life. He knows it isn't always going to be like this.

When He says, "I will never leave you nor forsake you," that's not just one of those comforting verses you can put in your pocket for a rainy day. What He's saying is, "I'm going to walk with you every day. I have an agenda and a plan, and I won't abandon the process for a single day. I'm going to be on the job every moment of your life, working to bring it to pass. I'm going to supervise this job. I'm going to be involved in its construction to every degree."

Through all that happens to me, whether good or bad, helpful or hurtful, blessing or burden, He is gradually conforming me into the very image of His Son (Romans

8:28-29). Day by day, hour by hour, He is shaping me to look like Jesus.

Why else should I put my hope in Him?

2. Because He hears my prayers

A woman prayed for her son three times a day. On one of the blank pages in her Bible, she listed the sins that were breaking her heart: drugs, disobedience, stealing, hate, mocking his mother, belittling his mother.

Knowing of her faith, a few of her acquaintances spoke unkindly to her. "Where is God?" they asked her. "Has He forgotten about you?" But this mother kept on praying, believing God was in control, and that He would hear her prayer.

The day came when her faith was rewarded. Her son accepted Jesus Christ and his life dramatically changed. This faithful mother opened her Bible to the page where she had listed her son's sins and rebellion and drew a red cross all the way through the list. Then she gave the Bible to her son.

Because of Christmas, because of Calvary, because of the Resurrection, those of us who belong to Jesus Christ have direct access to the throne of God (Hebrews 4:14-16). The Bible says we may come before our Father with confidence, receiving mercy and finding grace to help us in our time of need.

Why else should we fix our hope on the Lord?

3. Because He knows exactly what we need
When you and I choose a Christmas gift for a loved one, we ask ourselves, *What does this person need? What would he or she really desire? What would be special?* It isn't easy, is it? So often—though we try so hard—we miss the mark. But when you really "hit it," when your gift truly delights someone and speaks to them of your love and care, it makes it all worthwhile.

Not long ago, someone made a "hit" with Joyce and me. A couple from our church gave us an exquisite handmade nativity set. It is so delicate, so finely crafted that it takes your breath away. Each little figurine is clothed in tiny hand-stitched garments. The little sheep have real wool. It's so life-like that you feel as if you could close your eyes and step right into the scene. Joyce carefully and tenderly packs it away each year in cotton, and it's the first thing she takes out when the Christmas season arrives.

You see, those people knew how much we love nativity scenes. And because they love us, they handmade each little piece. It's masterful. It's a treasure. And every year it speaks to us of their love.

They *knew* this would be special. They knew it would be "just right" for Ron and Joyce Mehl as they crafted it for us.

The reason we can have hope is not just because God has an agenda and a plan, not just because He hears our prayers, but because He knows precisely what we need. He knows what to give me. He knows that my needs this year are different from last year's. He knows what would encourage my heart and bring me lasting joy.

When the prophet Elijah went through a period of exhaustion and deep depression in his ministry, the Lord tenderly ministered to him with the very gifts he needed at that moment. He sent an angel to bake a cake for him and serve him some cool water. Then he gave him a significant task to accomplish. He blessed the weary prophet with a fresh revelation of Himself. And finally, he gave him a friend and companion named Elisha, who would walk with him until the day of his home-going.

The Lord knows your needs too—right at this very moment. He knows when you need refreshment. He knows when you need a task to accomplish for the kingdom. He knows when you need a word of encouragement from on high. He knows when you long for a helping hand. And He knows when you just need a good friend who will walk with you and help shoulder your load. James wrote:

> Every good and perfect gift is from above, coming down from the Father of the heavenly lights, who does not change like shifting shadows.
> (James 1:17)

Why else should I place the full weight of my hope in the Lord?

4. Because He will show me how to be a source of hope to others
Paul wrote: "May the God of hope fill you with all joy and peace as you trust in him, so that you may *overflow* with hope by the power of the Holy Spirit" (Romans 15:13, emphasis added).

An elderly gentleman got on a bus with a pretty bouquet of flowers. He was looking for a seat, but the bus was very crowded. He saw one seat in the back, so he made his way down the aisle and sat down next to a teenage girl.

As he got closer, he noticed the girl was quietly weeping. He sat down and didn't say anything, but he was concerned for this young woman who was obviously distressed about something.

They rode along in silence until the bus neared his stop. Then he turned to the young woman and said, "These flowers are for my wife, but...I know she'd want you to have them. I thought they might cheer you up and brighten your day."

The young woman reluctantly took them, seeing the sincerity in the old man's face. She watched as he got off the bus...and walked slowly into the cemetery.

Healing in our heart happens often when we look beyond our own pain and hurt and seek to help others. When we pour hope out of our lives into the lives of others, we never have to worry about a shortfall. The God of hope fills us up again—to overflowing—with a fresh supply.

A Package Deal

The hope Jesus brought to planet Earth when He arrived in a Bethlehem manger was confirmed and made eternal when He later arose from a borrowed tomb after being crucified for our sins. And yet we don't always see it that way.

We are often like the two men on their way to the village of Emmaus, spoken of in Luke 24. Jesus had been crucified three days before, and these men were emotionally crushed. As they walked along the road and discussed the awful events of the past few days, Jesus Himself came up and started speaking to them—but Luke says they were "kept from recognizing him" (verse 16). When the Lord asked what they were talking about, they began to describe what had happened to Jesus. "We had hoped that he was the one who was going to redeem Israel," they said, making it clear their hope had died along with their leader.

Since we know the end of the story, we're tempted to shout, "Fellas, open your eyes! Jesus isn't dead—in fact, He's right there with you! Your hope is walking right beside you! Open your eyes!"

Not bad advice—for them or ourselves.

You see, Jesus came to bring us hope, and He died and rose again to make that hope spring eternal in our hearts. Christmas and Easter are a package deal!

And both, together, prove that love will always find a way.

CHAPTER ELEVEN

Love Found a Way...
to Bring Us Home

When God brings his firstborn into the world, he says,
"Let all God's angels worship him."

HEBREWS 1:6

Remember the old Bing Crosby number, "I'll Be Home for Christmas"?

When the celebrated crooner sang the tune, it came out smooth as eggnog...and rich with nostalgia.

> I'll be home for Christmas
> You can count on me
> Please have snow and mistletoe
> And presents on the tree....[1]

Being "home for Christmas" is one of the most wistful subjects we might think about. Many older saints who can't remember much about what happened last year, last week, or even last night, remember with crystal clarity childhood Christmases from fifty, sixty, even seventy years ago.

To this day, they can close their eyes and feel wet

snowflakes on upraised faces. They can hear tunes from a tiny music box that hasn't played in three quarters of a century. They can taste the candy canes, the wassail, the Christmas pudding—or the rare, succulent oranges they found in the bottom of a Christmas stocking. They can remember an expedition into the woods on a see-your-breath frosty morning to chop down a little tree—and decorating it with strings of cranberries or popcorn or paper chains or whatever they had on hand.

Oh so clearly they recall the excitement, the family gatherings, the caroling, the special doll with button eyes, the shiny new skates, or the little red wagon—childish hopes richly fulfilled or dashed.

Others recall homesick Christmases in faraway places…standing on the windswept deck of a destroyer in the cold North Atlantic during World War II…crouched in a bunker in steamy Southeast Asia…stuck in a lonely city hospital room…languishing at a job site in some desolate part of the country—with no money for a ticket home.

I remember the empty, lonely feeling I had as a Bible college freshman as the students emptied out of the dorm to head home for Christmas vacation. I wanted to go home too! But it's a long, long way from Los Angeles to Bloomington, Minnesota. (Sounds like a country-western song, doesn't it?) And I knew very well there was no money in the family kitty to spend on bus tickets. It was a miracle that I'd even come up with money for tuition and books.

I can see it so well in my mind's eye. I was all alone in the foyer of the men's dorm—now silent as a tomb—absently leafing through a magazine, feeling as lonely and homesick as I could. Christmas memories played across the screen of my mind, and that didn't help at all.

Suddenly Dr. Eno, our dorm "dad," strode into the room.

"Oh, there you are," he said, with a little twinkle in his eye. "Got something for you." He walked over to where I was sitting and handed me a sealed envelope. "Someone left this for you on the counter," he said. "Merry Christmas, son." And with that he walked out of the room.

When I opened the card, I could hardly believe my eyes. It contained a round-trip Greyhound ticket to Minneapolis. It was signed, in a handwriting I didn't recognize, "Someone who loves you."

But who did I know in Los Angeles? Who would do such a thing for a shy, skinny freshman from Minnesota? I went up to my room to pack, tears of gratitude beginning to well up in my eyes.

Somehow love had found a way to bring me home.

Others of us may have grown up in situations where "home for Christmas" wasn't a heartwarming prospect at all. There may have been strife, old family feuds, alcoholism, divorce, or illness, and the memories—well, they aren't what we wish they were.

But someday you and I will be home for Christmas.

Really home.

All the way home.

Home in heaven with our Lord Jesus. Home with the Christ of Christmas to celebrate His day with Him. How I anticipate that time! I find myself feeling homesick for a heavenly home I've never even seen.

With Him Where He Is

The Lord Jesus anticipates that day too. In the presence of His disciples He prayed, "Father, I want those you have given me to be with me where I am, and to see my glory, the glory you have given me because you loved me before the creation of the world" (John 17:24).

He wanted me to be with Him where *He* was...so He came down to where *I* was and made a way for me.

Recently I read about an incident in the life of Bud Wood, the founder of what has become one of the finest homes for mentally challenged children and adults. It's called Shepherd's Home and is in Union Grove, Wisconsin. In that facility, they care and minister to many children with Down's syndrome.

The staff at Shepherd's Home makes a concentrated effort to present the gospel to their residents. As a result, many of those at the home have come to faith in Jesus Christ. They have learned how deeply Jesus loves them and that He wants to make them whole and be with them forever. In fact,

He has prepared a place for them in His home in heaven and could return from the sky at any moment to take them there.

On a tour of the home with a friend, Bud happened to remark that one of the greatest daily maintenance problems the staff faces is smudged windows.

"Smudged windows?" his friend asked. "Why is that?"

Bud smiled and said, "You can walk through Shepherd's Home any time of day, and you will see some of these children standing with their hands, noses, and faces pressed to the glass."

Looking over at his perplexed friend, Bud added, "They're watching for Jesus. They keep checking to see if Christ is coming back yet—to take them to heaven."

The simple minds and hearts of these brothers and sisters ought to teach you and me to glance up once in a while…to see if Jesus might be on His way to take us home.[2]

Christmas in Heaven?

Will there be Christmas in heaven? Have you ever thought about it? Time, of course, as we know it, will no longer exist. There will be no need of calendars or clocks to mark the passing of time, because we will exist in one eternal *now*.

I'm not sure how Christmas could happen, since there will be no December—no turning of years. But I do know that God desires to honor His Son throughout all eternity. I do know that the angels will always be praising Him. And I also understand that you and I will be singing the song of the Lamb in full voice with great joy. Tidings of comfort and joy? You'd better believe it!

Why *not* honor Jesus for the time He stepped out of heaven to become a Man? He Himself will be wearing human flesh—including the scars in His hands, feet, and side—for all eternity as a reminder of what He suffered for us. Why shouldn't there be a remembrance of that remarkable moment (in earth time) when the Son of God humbled Himself and became a little baby, born to a simple Jewish girl in a little village called Bethlehem?

Why not?

You and I celebrate Christmas from an earthly point of view. From our perspective, He came down to us, lived among us for a time, died in our place, then ascended back into heaven. But what would those events look like from an angel's perspective?

We mark His coming; they watched Him leave.

We celebrate His arrival; they remember His departure.

We rejoice because of His presence; they experienced His absence.

We note that He left earth and ascended; they welcomed Him home.

Why shouldn't heaven celebrate His First Advent? Men and women could honor the day He came to earth; angels could honor the day He returned to glory. And why shouldn't there be decorations? An angel (a real one) on top of a great tree? Lights on the Tree of Life? Carol singing along the streets of gold? How about a gift exchange in honor of God's unspeakable gift that brought us to heaven?

My imagination runs away with me, but…I tend to think Christmas will be acknowledged somehow—as well as an Easter so full of thunderous joy I can't even conceive of it. Those were the events that made it possible for love to find a way.

It's Not a Dream

> Christmas Eve will find me
> Where the love light gleams
> I'll be home for Christmas
> If only in my dreams.[3]

But heaven is not a dream. It's a reality more solid than anything we've ever experienced in our life here on earth. The "love light" won't merely gleam, like a glint of colored light off a strand of tinsel, it will *blaze*. The light of the Lamb will illumine the new heaven and the new earth forever and ever.

Home won't be "only in your dreams." It will be real. The Son of God truly is going to take you home. He is preparing a place for you and me. In a sense, He "prepared a place" for us by going to the cross and enduring the penalty meant for you and me. There would be no thought or hope of a heavenly home if God had not given His only begotten Son.

Dr. Duffield, an elderly pastor and teacher much loved during his life, liked to tell the story about the elderly lady who, before she died, asked to be buried with a Bible under her arm and a fork in her hand.

The Bible symbolized her deep love for the Word of God. And the fork? She explained it like this. Whenever she went to a church potluck, she noticed that after the meal they picked up the plates but always said, "Keep your fork. The best is yet to come." She used to tell her children and grandchildren, "You can eat Jell-O with a spoon, but you can eat apple pie only with a fork."

So she was buried with her fork. It was her way of saying, "Don't grieve for me. I'm eating apple pie. I'm enjoying the very, very best."

I preached at Dr. Duffield's funeral not long ago. Not many people knew it, but as they closed the casket, his grandkids slipped in their grandfather's Bible...and a fork.

Before leaving the casket, they prayed together and one of them said, "God gave Pops a long life. But the best is yet to come." Their grandfather had preached about the love of God for many years, but now He was enjoying that love in all its immediacy and fullness. He had preached Christ through his whole career, but now was with the Lord Jesus— in His very presence.

The Best Is Yet to Come

Being a believer makes life here on earth about as good as it can be. In His love, God has found a way to bring us salvation, help, hope, counsel, joy—and more blessings than we can count.

But the best is yet to come. We will live with Him, walk with Him, speak with Him, and rule and reign with Him forever and ever.

So save your fork! The apple pie's on the way. We'll all be home for Christmas…and it won't be in our dreams.

CHAPTER TWELVE

He Will Always Find a Way

Thanks be to God for his indescribable gift!

2 CORINTHIANS 9:15

The message of Christmas is this: If by the birth of Jesus the love of God found a way to break into space and time and bring light, life, salvation, hope, joy, and help into our lives, *then no barrier in your life can frustrate Him.*

Isaiah prophesied:

> There will be no more gloom for those who were in distress....
>
> The people walking in darkness
> have seen a great light;
> on those living in the land of the shadow of death
> a light has dawned. (Isaiah 9:1-2)

When Jesus came, it was as though a mighty light from heaven broke through darkness, gloom, and shadow.

"Breaking through" is what His love is all about. It will break through *anything* to find you and touch you.

Nothing can stop Him from getting to the door of your heart.

If the almighty, eternal Son of God had to become a human being, He would do it. He would lay aside His mighty power and the splendor of His majesty and come into His own creation as a tiny baby.

And He did.

If He had to face down Satan and the jeering, slithering powers of hell, rejecting their temptations to shortcut the process (grabbing the reins of kingdom power but leaving us behind)—He would oppose them to the end.

And He did.

If He had to endure rejection, humiliation, mocking, and scorn, becoming a "man of sorrows, acquainted with grief," He would do it.

And He did.

If He had to die on a Roman cross for our sins, He would do it. If He had to drink the full cup of God's wrath for our sins, He would drink it. If He had to taste death in order to free us from the power of death, He would submit to it.

And He did.

Nothing stopped Him from bringing His message and accomplishing His mission. Not tradition. Not distance. Not darkness. Not Satan. Not hell. Not pain. Not even death itself.

How Did He Do That?

Wouldn't you have loved to have been in the room that Sunday night as the disciples huddled behind locked doors? Scripture records it like this:

> On the evening of that first day of the week, when the disciples were together, with the doors locked for fear of the Jews, Jesus came and stood among them and said, "Peace be with you!" After he said this, he showed them his hands and side. The disciples were overjoyed when they saw the Lord.
>
> Again Jesus said, "Peace be with you! As the Father has sent me, I am sending you." (John 20:19-21)

How had He found them? How had He passed through locked doors without opening them? *How had He emerged from the tomb alive?*

He found a way. He always does. He will do anything, go anywhere, fight any battle, oppose any foe, move any mountain, walk through any storm, roll away any stone. Nothing can keep His love from touching your heart...but you.

There is no door in the universe that can keep Him out. And yet...if you turn Him away from your own heart's door,

He will not come in. If you choose to spurn His love and reject His gift of eternal life, He will not force it upon you. In Revelation 3:20, the Lord Jesus says, "Here I am! I stand at the door and knock. If anyone hears my voice and opens the door, I will come in and eat with him, and he with me."

If you open the door the smallest crack, if you turn to Him, if you begin to seek Him, if you begin to long after Him in your heart, He'll find a way to get through to you.

Some dear friends of ours, Pastor and Mrs. Claude Updike, went on a trip to some distant Pacific islands. Pastor Updike, who told people about Christ wherever he went, found himself walking one late afternoon through a poor village. At the end of a long dirt road, he walked up to a humble little house and greeted an elderly couple, sitting on their porch and enjoying the little breeze off the ocean.

Brother Updike began to witness to this couple. "Did you know that God sent His own Son to save you and bring you eternal life? Did you know that Jesus loves you and has come to bring you great joy?"

The old man looked at his wife. "See?" he said. "It's just like I told you. If there really was a God, He'd send someone to tell us."

It doesn't matter where you are in this wide world of ours; you might be under the polar icecap in a nuclear submarine or orbiting the planet in the space shuttle. Call Him and He'll come.

It doesn't matter what you've done in your life, how

deeply and grievously you have sinned, how often you have failed, or how many people oppose you. Call on His name and He will save you.

It doesn't matter what your circumstances or situation might be; whether you are in gravest danger or in a long, flat, dreary stretch of life that seems to go on and on with no end in sight. Reach out your hand and He will grip it.

This is a love that will track you into the swamps, through the valleys, across the deserts, and over the jagged mountain peaks. It will follow you and call to you and whisper your name through the long years. Your heart may become cold as ice or hard as stone, but His love—the full, radiant, powerful love of your Creator and Redeemer—will be as near to you as it has always been.

Breathe His name and He is there.

Say the word and He'll show you.

Even right now.

Love will find a way.

Notes

Chapter Two: Love Found a Way…to Save Us

1. Arthur John Gossip, in *Classic Sermons on the Attributes of God,* comp. Warren W. Wiersbe (Grand Rapids, Mich.: Kregel, 1989), 148-9.

2. Edward Payson, *Memoir, Select Thoughts and Sermons* (reprint, Harrisonburg, Va.: Sprinkle Publications, 1988), 500-1.

Chapter Five: Love Found a Way…to Bring Us Joy

1. Source unknown

Chapter Six: Love Found a Way…to Counsel Us

1. "Jesus We Crown You with Praise" by Lanny Wolfe. © Copyright 1994. Lanny Wolfe Music/ASCAP (admin. by ICG). All rights reserved. Used by permission.

2. *Mathew Henry's Commentary on the Whole Bible: New Modern Edition Electronic Database* (Peabody, Mass.: Hendrickson Publishers, Inc., 1991). Used by permission. All rights reserved.

Chapter Ten: Love Found a Way...to Bring Us Hope

1. Charles R. Swindoll, *The Tale of the Tardy Oxcart and 1,501 Other Stories* (Nashville: Word, 1998), 275, with added detail from a sermon by Mike Macintosh, Horizon Christian Fellowship, San Diego, California.

Chapter Eleven: Love Found a Way...to Bring Us Home

1. "I'll Be Home for Christmas," by Kim Gannon, Walter Kent, and Buck Ram. Reprinted by permission of Gannon and Kent Music Co., copyright 1943, renewed 1971.

2. This story was adapted from Joseph Stowell, *Eternity* (Chicago: Moody Press, 1997), 122-3.

3. "I'll Be Home for Christmas," by Gannon, Kent, and Ram.